Stream Smallmouth Fishing

Stream Smallmouth Fishing

Tim Holschlag

Stackpole Books

Published by
STACKPOLE BOOKS
Cameron and Kelker Streets
P.O. Box 1831
Harrisburg, PA 17105

Printed in the United States of America

10 9 8 7 6 5 4 3 2 1

First Edition

Illustrations by Betsy Kenney
Cover design by Tracy Patterson
Cover photograph by Lyn Verthein
Interior design by Ellen Dawson

On the cover: Two nice stream smallmouth caught on a single cast by the author. These
and other fish pictured in the book were released after posing.

Library of Congress Cataloging-in-Publication Data

Holschlag, Tim, 1950–
    Stream smallmouth fishing / Tim Holschlag – 1st ed.
        p.   cm.
    Includes index.
    ISBN 0-8117-2384-4
    1. Smallmouth bass fishing.   I. Title.
SH681.H618   1990
799.1'758 – dc20   90-31614
                                                                        CIP

Contents

Acknowledgments

FEW BOOKS are solely the property of one person, and this one is certainly no exception. More state and provincial fisheries department professionals than I can mention, from across the smallmouth's range, contributed their knowledge of smallmouth bass and their habits. Likewise, I must acknowledge the input of the many smallmouth anglers whose experiences I have shared over the years. In particular, I want to acknowledge several individuals whose ideas contributed significantly to the book. A sincere thank-you to Smallmouth Alliance organizer Kurt Sleighter, to float-fishing expert Sheldon Bolstad, and to longtime smallmouth addict and good friend Dan Johnson. Another acknowledgment to out-door writer and fly-fishing expert Greg Breining. Most of all I want to thank Lyn, my partner in life's adventures; her patience, support, and editing skills are truly enormous.

Introduction

OVER THE YEARS, I have often wondered why so many fishing writers, and even many anglers themselves, have overlooked stream smallmouth bass fishing. This continued neglect seems particularly odd considering the rise in popularity of the smallmouth nationally over the past decade. But in significant areas of the smallmouth's range, fishing in rivers and creeks is still largely overlooked. If any outdoor writers do mention stream bass fishing, they lump all rivers together, no matter how different. Many anglers also seem unaware of stream fishing, even though this tremendous fisheries resource encompasses well over 25,000 stream miles from New Brunswick to Arkansas, many times almost under our noses.

Stream fishing is very different from the increasingly technological and mechanized (and crowded) lake angling of today. You don't have to journey to remote Canadian waters or fight the crowds on a big-name lake to find the "gamest fish that swims," as J. A. Henshall, one of the pioneers of American angling, called the smallmouth. Even if many of the pros are busy zooming across Lake Erie or Dale Hollow Reservoir, I believe it's time to discover our continent's stream smallmouth. That's what this book is all about. It gives you solid advice on tactics and techniques to find and catch stream bass (and other stream species). This book is directed completely toward stream fishing and is based on many years of stream-fishing experience.

In the broadest sense, I've tried to write for everyone interested in fishing, especially on our moving waters. More specifically, this book is for three particular groups of people – besides already committed stream fishers. First, lake anglers who spend considerable time every year chasing bass, walleye, or such. If you are frustrated with the increasing crowds and decreasing fish, or tired of needing $25,000 worth of hardware to be considered a respectable angler, this book, my friends, is definitely for you.

The second group is stream trout fans, you stout-hearted souls who already know the genuine excitement to be found around the next creek bend or in the next pool. I ask you to consider trying another form of stream angling that will add a new dimension to your fishing enjoyment (not least because of the smallmouth's ability to fight circles around the brown trout or brookie).

Finally, this is for that growing army of fitness-oriented folks, those of you who enjoy fishing but think that fitness and today's fishing are miles apart, especially when you see all those guys with "spare tires" coming back to the boat landing in their 150-horsepower machines. Stream fishing could very well be for you. I know of no better sport for keeping a person fit (both physically and mentally) than a regular program of stream angling. If you want a fishing experience close to nature (something I believe most of us enjoy), try slipping along a quiet wooded creek and listening to the melody of a song sparrow while you watch a family of wood ducks work their way downstream. It's hard to beat.

I have tried not to include misleading generalizations that come primarily from lake fishing. The methods and techniques described here have been personally tested on many streams over many years. I have been pursuing the wily stream smallmouth for over a quarter century. During this time I've caught (and released) more than 8,000 smallmouth from more than 125 U.S. and Canadian rivers – not to mention the thousands of "bonus" fish (like walleye, trout, catfish, and pickerel) from these same waters.

Over the years I have fished for many different species in many different settings, but my first love was (and still is) stream smallmouth. My interest in our streams and their inhabitants has meant many thousands of fishing hours, with more sixteen-hour days spent wading, walking, or floating than I should admit. Year by year, stream by stream, and fish by fish, I've compiled a body of angling knowledge that I hope will help make your fishing much more productive and enjoyable.

1 ⌒

Why Stream Fishing?

IT WAS A WARM SATURDAY AFTERNOON in late July, and I was nearly waist deep in a clear rock- and gravel-bottomed stream not far from a city of 100,000 people. Since the weather and the water were both so warm, I was wading in shorts and sandals. The water felt good. Wet wading is a little like swimming while you're fishing. More important, I was fishing – and catching fish. Flipping my homemade spinner-fly upstream along an undercut bank, I almost immediately received a hard strike, the fifth in as many casts. This last fish turned into a hard-fighting, high-jumping 14-inch small-mouth that strained my 7-foot light-action rod to its fullest for several minutes until brought to hand. This red-eyed bronze beauty was only one of nineteen bass, five walleye, and six rock bass I caught and released that sunny afternoon. The real beauty of it all was that this outstanding fishing took place on an accessible stream close to a major population center on the weekend, and without another angler in sight. Best of all, this experience was no rare fluke. I have had literally hundreds of other equally enjoyable stream fishing outings in the past thirty years, from Oklahoma to Virginia.

Let's pause for a brief definition. In my mind, a smallmouth stream is any of the many rivers or creeks that can't be easily fished by large boats, and must be either waded or floated by smaller watercraft such as canoes or johnboats. These waterways may be only a few yards wide and 4 feet deep in their pools. They are often

Young and old, male and female—everyone can enjoy stream fishing.

tributaries of larger rivers and have water at least slightly warmer than the cooler trout streams. They also contain enough of a proper substrate (bottom) and adequate water quality to maintain a permanent, naturally reproducing, self-sustaining bass population. (In this book the term "bass," unless stated otherwise, means smallmouth bass.)

Stream smallmouth fishing is very different from motoring down the mighty Mississippi or Ohio River, whose depths commonly reach more than 10 feet. Stream angling, where depths are often well under 7 feet, calls for different skills and equipment and a whole different approach; any would-be stream angler should recognize this. Without proper stream techniques, even a good deep-river fisher will never become more than a marginal stream angler. While on the subject, I should also say that to me smallmouth fishing doesn't mean sitting on a bank all day soaking a night-crawler and hooking whatever species happens by. Stream smallmouth angling, just like lake bassing or stream trout fishing, requires a wide range of techniques and tactics to be consistently successful.

In the lake-rich parts of the country many anglers have only limited knowledge about the ribbons of water they drive across on their way to the lake. In some areas of the eastern United States where there are fewer lakes, the tradition of hitting the rivers for the mighty smallmouth is fairly strong, but even those anglers often overlook the smaller waters in their areas.

This wasn't always so. Forty years ago stream fishing had quite a following. But with the creation of more lakes and a better road system to get to them, interest in streams declined. Today, once again, things are changing, and moving waters are receiving renewed interest and attention. Many anglers are looking for something more than the crowded, overfished lakes and are discovering the many advantages of stream fishing.

Why stream fishing? What does it have going for it that warrants your interest as an angler? The fact is that many warm-water (nontrout) streams have fisheries that are almost completely unused for sport fishing.

Almost every smallmouth region in the country has dozens of lesser-known streams where a good angler can catch twenty-five to thirty bass plus ten to fifteen other fish a day. We're talking here of smallmouth mainly between 10 and 15 inches, with a good possibility of catching real dandies of 16 to 18 inches and the occasional giant of 20 inches or more. The "nice" fish of, say, 12 inches will be around a pound in weight and will fight with tremendous speed, high jumps, and phenomenal staying power. On those streams with high populations of smaller bass (under 10 inches), catches of over forty a day are easy. After years of catching thousands of fish of many species, I will argue that a stream smallmouth on light tackle is, pound for pound, the hardest-fighting fish in fresh water. No words can really describe the fight of a 15-inch summer smallmouth on the end of a light spinning or fly rod. I can only hope you experience it for yourself.

Many warm-water streams that contain bass also offer plentiful numbers of pickerel or pike, walleye, rock bass, sunfish, hard-fighting catfish, and even muskies—all lightly fished. This includes even many very small rivers that most anglers think are unable to sustain these species. Some of these "trickles," in fact, have more of these other fish than they have bass. All these fish thrive in these fairly restricted habitats because of the lack of fishing pressure or, more accurately, the lack of fish-*killing* pressure. The truth is that no smallmouth stream can support high numbers of larger fish being killed. The amount of habitat is quite limited and the growth rate of the fish is generally slow. It takes most stream smallmouth well over three years to reach one pound and over five years to make the 2-pound mark. This leaves us with only two choices: either we can kill these fish off today and ruin our fishing for tomorrow, or we can release them so we will continue to have good fishing tomorrow and the next day. If a significant number of anglers start fishing a stream and *keeping* the larger fish, these fragile fisheries will be depleted.

Recycling (catch and release) is the only way to go for these waters. Practicing this simple, free, and satisfying conservation method will significantly help keep our waterways full of bass, especially bigger bass. Every year, I catch hundreds of smallmouth and release them all. Not keeping them doesn't lessen my fishing pleasure. On the contrary, *knowing* there is an 18-inch lunker in a spot because I released her there last week makes today's fishing much more exciting and enjoyable.

Enjoyment is still what fishing is all about. And it isn't

measured solely by poundage of fish killed or caught. Many other factors add to the sense of feeling happy at the end of the fishing day – things like the relative solitude, abundance of wildlife, and the physical exercise involved in stream fishing.

Almost all stream fishing, be it for bass, trout, or whatever, puts the angler much closer to the environment than the boat-bound lake fisher. Standing knee-deep in a softly murmuring brook on an early summer evening affects all your senses. Feeling the stream rush through the riffle and curl around the bend actually makes you a part of the stream environment. It isn't easy to explain why moving water has such an attraction for the river devotee. Maybe it's because of the ever-changing nature of the stream, with its continuously moving water bringing a new environment each minute, while at the same time seeming to remain the same. Just watching this change, feeling this continuous passing as the entire river drifts by you, is both soothing and mystifying. Part of the attraction is also the sound of the water, at times barely a whisper

Streamside camping while on a fishing float trip is a great way to enjoy our river resources.

and other times almost a roar. And there is the quality of mystery. As the twisting and winding ribbon of moving water quickly disappears around the bend, what lies beyond? What mother lode of fish is just upstream, waiting to be discovered? Following that ever-moving trail of water can easily become a goal in itself.

Smallmouth streams often run through the most scenic areas. Much of Oklahoma is arid and bare, but the smallmouth streams on the east side of the state flow through beautiful wooded hills. Get on the smallie waters of eastern Iowa with their limestone outcroppings and you'll have trouble believing you are really in an agricultural state. Heavily populated Pennsylvania has dozens of streams that amaze and delight new anglers with their beauty and tranquility. And of course the rugged scenery surrounding Arkansas, Tennessee, and West Virginia mountain streams is the stuff of picture postcards. Virtually all other states and provinces that have smallmouth rivers also have streams where you can get away from the crowds, clear your mind, and soothe your eyes with pleasing sights.

Pursuing these subtler aspects of stream fishing necessitates a very definite use of physical energy. I consider this a very good thing. Instead of a rigorous (and boring) exercise program, why not get rid of those "spare tires" (and keep them off) while really enjoying yourself? Any stream angling (be it on foot or by watercraft) enables you to get more exercise than motorized boat fishing, and it's a lot more fun than jogging. Actually feeling the river bottom under your feet as you wade through the shallows, or pushing the alder bushes aside as you move softly along the bank, is a satisfying physical experience. So is feeling your paddle dig into the water of a slow pool. It feels good at the end of the day to know you covered those miles. Start out with easy sections of water, and by the end of the season not only should the streams be easier, but those three flights of stairs at work you used to huff and puff over should also be a snap.

One of the best fringe benefits of stream fishing is the intimate contact with the wonders of nature, offering many opportunities to increase your enjoyment. Amateur ornithology (bird watching) is a fine way to get more out of your fishing. In fact, during some trips in the spring my binoculars and bird book get nearly as much of a workout as my rod. Identifying the profusion of beautiful wildflowers that inhabit nearly every riverbank will keep you busy for years. How about mycology (mushrooming)? Almost everywhere, many delicious varieties of mushrooms grow literally under your feet on the banks. Other people also enjoy geology (including rock hunting), tree identification, or nature photography. And, of course, you will see much more of the larger wildlife along the streams. Is seeing a young woodchuck trying to climb a sapling to reach its leaves as enjoyable as catching a bass? Is watching a whitetail doe and fawn quietly cross the creek right in front of you as thrilling as hooking a nice fish? You will have to judge these experiences for yourself. I know I remember and treasure those moments just as much as my actual fishing experiences.

2

Identifying and Exploring Smallmouth Streams

THE FIRST SECTION of this chapter describes the basic characteristics of smallmouth streams. Knowing more about the needs and habitat of river smallmouth bass will make fishing more interesting and productive for everyone. And for those who want to expand their fishing horizons beyond their local streams, knowing how to identify more good waters is essential.

The second section of this chapter lists more than one hundred streams from thirty-one states and provinces, and tells how to find many other popular and lesser-known waters. It's a fact that nearly all smallmouth-producing states and provinces have streams that are almost unknown to anglers – and often lots of them. In these areas, if you want to try more streams, it will be up to you to identify and explore them. I'm not exaggerating on this point. There are literally thousands of miles of little-known smallmouth streams in the United States and Canada, and not just in remote wild areas. Many heavily populated states have numerous streams that receive little fishing pressure. Often the states' fishing communities are barely aware of them; even the fisheries departments have no accurate list of their states' smallmouth streams.

Why this enormous ignorance? In some states, the reasons are obvious. Anglers in Pennsylvania overlook numerous smallmouth streams because many are obsessed with trout, or they concentrate only on the larger "big name" bass rivers. Minnesota is

In the eastern half of the continent at least twenty-six states and three provinces have river smallmouth. Though smallmouth are newer to the West, a number of states have localized but expanding populations.

hooked on walleyes, and its fisheries department puts the bulk of its resources into walleye production to the neglect of other species. But some other states with much less total fishing possibilities don't pay much attention to many of their smallmouth waters either, and it's hard to figure out why. For some areas, it simply may be collective ignorance. Both individual anglers and fisheries professionals just don't know that there are hundreds of miles of smallie water untapped in their state. In some other areas, perhaps the anglers have become fixated on the newly created reservoirs and the mechanized type of fishing associated with these big lakes. Of course, lake angling *is* easier. Just buy a big, expensive rig and your exercise days are over. Besides, just look at the hordes of people on those lakes; with "everybody" out there, it must be the way to fish, right?

Exploring smallmouth streams may not be for everyone, but personally I think the adventure and satisfaction of "discovering" new waters is one of the more exciting things about stream angling. And precisely because almost everyone else is out there on the lake (or trout stream), bass streams are uncrowded, relatively untouched sources of quality fishing.

WHAT MAKES FOR A GOOD STREAM?

The best way to identify good smallmouth water is to know the main characteristics that combine to make up a smallmouth bass stream. This section will touch on only the most basic of these characteristics. The total ecosystem of a warm-water river is very complex, and a comprehensive understanding would take considerably more study than we have room for.

Bottom Type (Substrate)

Almost all good smallmouth streams contain moderate to high amounts of rocky substrate. (There are a few that contain smallmouth and very little rock, but they are exceptions.) In smallmouth streams, rocks are used as food larders, hiding places, and ambush cover. One reason rocks are so important for good fish populations is that crawfish (a major bass food) depend on rocky bottoms. In fact, during the peak summer growing period the smallmouth's diet is as much as 80 percent crawfish. Without this high amount of crawfish, the bass population in the stream would quickly decline.

When it comes to good smallmouth rocks, not all stones are created equal. Cobble (fist to football-sized rock) is best for food production, so good streams should have plentiful amounts of stones of this size. A smaller percentage of much larger rock is also important for optimum bass habitat. Large boulders several feet in diameter are good as hiding spots and as current buffers. In some streams, large downed trees act as substitutes. Banks lined with riprap (rock or broken concrete) to prevent erosion often benefit fish populations. In a badly silted-in stream, properly placed riprap (where the current keeps the rock from silting over) is often the best place to find smallmouth. Huge car-sized boulders or slab rock protruding from the water may look dramatic, but they aren't very good fish habitat. A stream bottom of *mostly* large, flat rock (like unbroken, smooth limestone) is a fairly barren habitat for smallmouth food – and thus for the bass themselves.

The worst kinds of stream substrates are soft silt and sifting sand, which hold little food for bass. In areas where the land is very sandy some natural sand erosion will occur, but streams that have very high amounts of sand or soft silt (dirt) probably suffer from human-caused erosion. Heavy agricultural production nearby is the

A testimony to the beauty and productivity of limestone streams. Lyn Verthein.

major cause of silted-in streams. One word of caution about silty streams: even waterways that receive only a moderate amount of fine silt will run very turbid because this material stays suspended in the water for so long, but many of these streams are still good bass waters. Don't automatically assume that low-visibility water means no rocky substrate and poor bass fishing. Sometimes the only way you can tell if a low-visibility stream still has a rock bottom is by probing it with a paddle or long pole.

Size of the Stream

The widths and depths of a stream and the amount of water it carries are easy to observe *at any one time.* But it's important to know what a stream's flow is like at different times of the year. Remember, bass must live in the stream year round (or at least from spring until fall). So, if a stream almost dries up in late summer it won't be a productive stream even if its spring flows seem fine. A minimum flow for a small bass creek is somewhere in the neighborhood of 5 to 10 cubic feet per second.

Many things influence how much water a stream carries, and the amount of rainfall isn't always the most important factor. Streams with a lot of marsh drainage have much more stable flows than those with ditched or straightened headwater creeks (which allow the water to drain rapidly). High amounts of spring seepage also make a stream run more stable. Human activity continues to upset the natural drainages of many streams, and those affected the least by wide flow fluctuations are generally the most productive.

Winter flow conditions are also very important to smallmouth. If a stream floods a great deal during the cold-water period and it doesn't have many deep-water boulders or logs, it will probably not support many bass. When water temperatures are in the mid-30s, smallmouth are extremely lethargic. They can't swim against a strong current and are swept downstream and killed if they can't escape strong flows. Streams with most of the deeper rocky pools silted in (probably due to agricultural erosion) are very susceptible to this type of winter kill. Many Illinois streams suffer from this problem. Winter kills caused by oxygen deprivation are less common. Fortunately, it does not take a lot of water flowing under the ice to keep the fish alive.

Gradient

The gradient of a stream (how much it drops per mile) significantly influences its overall productivity. With insufficient gradient, a stream is a sluggish largemouth river; too much drop, and the currents are too strong for smallies. Gradients ranging from 4 to 7 feet per mile seem to suit smallmouth best (although numerous rivers with higher or lower gradients certainly hold fish). The currents caused by these gradients accomplish several things (besides pushing your craft down the river), and a very important one is that they create pools and riffles. Flowing at the proper speed over rock and gravel substrates, water will scour out softer bottom material and create pools. When the moving water hits a harder bottom it can't wash away, it's forced to speed up over it. The result is shallow, well-oxygenated rocky riffles, which are common on most good waterways. These riffles are very rich in bass food.

Stream Fertility

The fertility of a stream determines how many fish the stream can support and how fast they grow. Fertility is determined by several factors, including size of stream, gradient, substrate, water temperature, and nearby land types. For instance, streams that warm up slowly in the spring and turn cool quickly in the fall tend to be infertile because of their short growing season.

Another major influence on fertility is the alkalinity of the water. In fact, just determining the alkalinity of a stream will tell you much of what you should know about its fertility. It seems high alkalinity, in the order of 150 parts per million (ppm) or more, allows for high production of invertebrates (aquatic insects and crawfish) and low alkalinity (below 40 ppm) limits their growth. Alkalinity is largely determined by the type of land and substrates the river flows through. Streams flowing through land with considerable limestone are quite high in alkalinity, while waters coming out of or through bogs are very low. Low alkalinity is the reason even some very rocky streams are poor smallmouth waters.

It's wise to find out if a stream's alkalinity has been measured. Check with your state or provincial fisheries department to see if they've surveyed the stream and measured alkalinity. Even without this technical information, a competent angler can uncover other evidence indicating a stream's alkalinity. A limestone stream, remember, is likely to be quite fertile. Another way to check is to look carefully for evidence of invertebrates and small baitfish. If a stream is quite fertile, these species will be in abundance. Carefully observing the shallows and overturning rocks in the riffles will tell you how much life there is in the waterway.

Food Sources

The diet of the river smallmouth bass consists of a variety of food sources, with the basic predator fish rules applying—they eat what is most available, is easiest to capture, and allows the best growth. This means that different foods are eaten in different streams and at different times of year. Looking at the fish's range as a whole, smallie food can be divided into four categories: aquatic insects (such as hellgrammites and caddisfly nymphs), small fish (such as minnows, chubs, and sculpins), crawfish, and "terrestrial" food (such as grasshoppers and frogs). However, the diet of most adult fish is 90 percent crawfish and small fish. An exception to this are small bass, who often consume significant amounts of aquatic insects.

Crawfish in particular play a great role, since they make up so much of the smallmouth's diet during the peak growth period of summer. In fact, rivers that have low crawfish populations seldom have high bass populations. Small fish, though generally less prominent in the bass's diet than crawfish, are still very important. In the spring and fall, when crawfish are scarce, the availability of easy meals of small fish is essential for a healthy population of bass. Even though the bass may not be growing significantly during the spring and fall, forage fish allow them to at least maintain their weight. Different species of forage fish are used in different streams, including several minnow species, chubs, shiners, and the bottom-dwelling mad toms and sculpins.

Reproductive Needs

All across their range, river smallmouth have very similar needs for successful reproduction: a water temperature of at least 60 degrees and a bottom substrate of coarse gravel or pebbles in 1 to 4 feet of

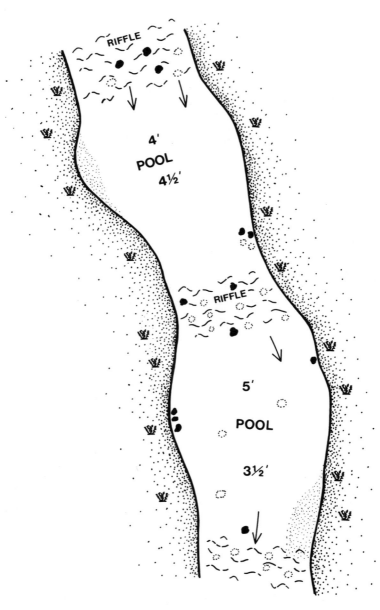

Representation of pool and riffle habitat. The rocky, well-oxygenated riffles produce large amounts of food for the bass; the pools provide safety, resting areas, and winter habitat.

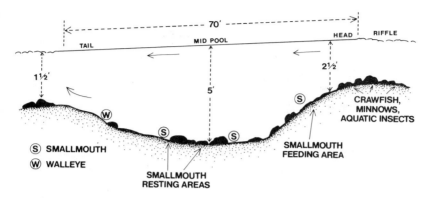

Side view of riffle/pool/riffle. The smallmouth at the head of the pool will be the most active. Those in the deepest part of the pool, while less active, can still be caught. So can fish in the tail of the pool. "S" designates smallmouth.

water that is protected from strong current flows. In some streams, successful spawning takes place almost every year, while in the poorest of bass waters reproduction may be terrible for four years running and then only fair during the fifth year.

Reproductive success is largely governed by how much flooding occurs during spawning. If a stream's flow is only low to moderate during spawning and the fish have access to good current blocks such as boulders or logs, reproduction will be good. If flooding occurs and few adequate current blocks are available, the numbers of smallmouth fry that survive will be negligible. Strong currents will sweep the fry away. This is the biggest factor that limits reproductive success, and it is often a human-caused problem. When streams experience high water and strong flows from even only modest rains, it is nearly always because of habitat problems — they have lost their natural vegetative cover or have had their feeder creeks straightened. Also, large amounts of sifting sand bottoms will limit reproduction.

Sometimes fish are able to overcome reproductive limitations by traveling up small creeks that have lots of good spawning substrate and do not easily flood. In some areas fish travel upstream as much as 30 miles to spawn in tributary streams. This is why dams blocking the spring spawning movement can lead to reduced spawning success in a particular river section. For spawning to be successful on larger waters *on a regular basis,* plenty of current-breaking obstructions are necessary in the spawning areas. If bass in large waterways have these large obstructions (probably large boulders) along shallow shorelines, spawning success can be fairly high. Good anglers can often tell if reproduction is regularly successful on a given river simply by taking careful note of the size fish they catch. If you *consistently* catch bass of many different sizes (year classes), it's a safe bet that spawning has been consistent for several years. Conversely, if there are large gaps in the size of the fish you catch, reproduction has probably been poor during some years.

All these factors together—substrate, stream size and flow, gradients, fertility, food sources, and spawning areas—make up a smallmouth stream. By looking for these characteristics, you can judge the fishing potential of any stream, and use this knowledge to aid you in exploring for more good smallmouth water.

FINDING SMALLMOUTH STREAMS

As the range map of river smallmouth shows, the finest fish in fresh water, as I call the smallmouth, inhabits nearly the entire eastern half of the United States and southern Canada. From Oklahoma to the Atlantic Ocean the bronzeback is native or has been firmly established. In twenty-six eastern states and three Canadian provinces, many hundreds of individual rivers and creeks contain fishable populations of smallmouth—well over 35,000 miles of moving water, ranging from tiny creeks you can jump across to river giants like the lower Susquehanna and the mighty Mississippi. They are crystal-clear waterways winding through near wilderness, coffee-colored streams in the Farm Belt, and rivers surrounded by major urban centers. No matter where you live in the eastern half of the country, the "finest fishing in fresh water" probably isn't far away, provided you know where (and how) to look for it. Even in the western portion of the United States, where smallies aren't native, they are being introduced into a growing number of waters. While not every western fisher has this type of fishing readily available, many do and more will in the future.

Below is a chart listing a few smallmouth waters in each state or province. Most of these streams are popular waterways that produce good to excellent fishing. For those who don't know of any other streams or have no desire to seek out lesser-known waters, these should provide you with a starting point. Since some states

Smallmouth Streams by Region and State

East

Connecticut – *Housatonic, Farmington, Connecticut*
Delaware – *Delaware*
Maine – *Kennebec, Union, Sandy, Belgrade Stream*
Massachusetts – *Nashua, Connecticut, Salmon*
Maryland – *Potomac, Patapsco, North Branch Potomac, Youghiogheny*
New Hampshire – *Contoocock, Merrimack, Pemigewasset*
New Jersey – *Delaware, Pohatcong*
New York – *Hudson, Mohawk, Susquehanna, Wallkill*
Pennsylvania – *Allegheny, Juniata, Pine, Susquehanna*
Vermont – *White, West, Connecticut*
Virginia – *James, Clinch, Rappahannock, Shenandoah*

Mid-South

Alabama – *Elk, Tennessee*
Arkansas – *Kings, Crooked Creek, War Eagle, Buffalo*
Kentucky – *Green, Nolin, Troublesome, State Creek*
Missouri – *Big Piney, Osage Fork, Niangua, Gasconade*
North Carolina – *New River, Little Tennessee*
Oklahoma – *Glover, Kiamichi, Flint, Little River, Mountain Fork*
Tennessee – *Watuga, Elk, Little Tennessee, Caney Fork*
West Virginia – *South Fork Potomac, Cacapon, New, Greenbrier*

Midwest

Indiana – *Big Blue, Sugar Creek, Elkhart, St. Joseph*
Illinois – *Sugar, Dupage, Apple, Kishwaukee*
Iowa – *Upper Iowa, Turkey, Winnebago, Middle Raccoon*
Michigan – *Grand, Thornapple, Paint, Huron*
Minnesota – *Kettle, Mississippi, Vermillion, Zumbro*
Ohio – *Paint, Greenville Creek, Stillwater, Sunfish*
Wisconsin – *Oconto, Red Cedar, Wisconsin, Grant*

Canada

Ontario – *St. Lawrence, Grand, Winnipeg*
New Brunswick – *St. Croix, Meduxnekeag, St. John*
Quebec – *Ottawa*

West

Oregon – *John Day, Umatilla, Umpqua, South Umpqua*
Washington – *Columbia, Yakima, Snake, Okanagan*
New Mexico – *Gila, Chama*
California – *Cache, Russian*

have more than one hundred smallmouth streams within their borders and many others have several dozen, this sampling of streams should be seen as just that – a sample of what is available.

Finding Relatively Well-Known Streams

Actually finding a variety of smallmouth waters causes some anglers difficulty – not because there aren't any streams available, but because they simply don't know where to look. Of course, if you want to spend your entire life on a single river, that's fine with me. But if you want to compile a good list of streams to fish, I'll give some tips on how to go about it.

Fisheries Commissions

When it comes to identifying streams to fish, the information available varies greatly from one state to another. Wherever you live, the first place to start is the state fisheries commission or department. Some states have a list of at least their better-known streams. Call or write to the fisheries state headquarters and ask if they have any river smallmouth guides. Even if they don't have a publication, ask if they can put you in touch with a knowledgeable official who could give you an oral list. Also find out if the state has recent fish population surveys (probably from electrofishing or creel surveys). This data will give some idea of where the fish are in the river, how many, and how big. Often state headquarters will refer you to regional offices. Gathering information from these smaller units can be time consuming, but they often have information the state headquarters do not have.

Outdoor Publications and Shops

Probably the next best source is local outdoor or fishing publications. Many magazines periodically run articles on where to go for bronzebacks, including numerous popular waters. These lists are seldom all-inclusive, but they'll point you to many good streams. Check back issues in the library. Next, try river-oriented tackle shops and canoe guides. With the growing popularity of canoeing, printed canoe guides are becoming common, and many of them at least mention the fishing available in the listed rivers.

Finding and Exploring Lesser-Known Streams

Smaller bass streams are very overlooked in many areas, and there are literally hundreds of them waiting to be discovered. If you want to expand your fishing horizons beyond the larger waters, you will have to take some initiative, but your efforts will be richly rewarded. Actually finding a nice stream that few others know about is enormously satisfying, and the process of exploring can be almost a goal in itself.

Basic Research

Where to start in snooping out these little-known waters? As with better-known rivers, your first stop should be the state fisheries commission. Don't expect a lot of easy information; settle for as many bits and pieces as you can get. Look at all the electrofishing data the state has on its smaller warm-water (nontrout) streams. Contact the regional fishery offices, find out who the most knowledgeable people are, and talk to them directly. Tell them that you like exploring new waters and ask if they can give you any tips on *little-known* streams in their district. Call some game wardens (enforcement personnel) and ask them the same thing. Don't be shy, and don't be quickly discouraged. Some may brush you off, but keep trying. Finding one or two knowledgeable and helpful people will make the effort worth it.

Another possible source of information is local bait shops. Well-chosen questions ("Doesn't anyone ever catch any bass out of Jones Creek?") may elicit valuable information. Local anglers in your targeted area can also provide you with some tips. Some may be reluctant to direct you to their favorite spots, but if you make it clear that you are a catch-and-release angler and aren't going to bring hordes of others to their spots, you can often get them to loosen up. Stop at stream access points—bridges, canoe launches, dams—and talk to people. By accumulating tidbits of information this way, you can start to assemble a valuable body of stream information.

Educated Exploration

Now comes the really fun part—the "field research." This is when you actually see for yourself what the streams are like. I call

Even large cities can offer good smallmouth angling nearby. Lyn Verthein.

this research "educated exploration," because without an organized and rational system, you'll spend a lot of time with little results.

A key ingredient of this type of research is getting good maps of the area you are interested in. I can't emphasize this too strongly. Without detailed county road maps or topographical maps (preferably both), you will be literally going in circles. Most states have very detailed county road maps that show all streams no matter how small, plus all roadways, bridges, and hamlets. Some even depict all dams, marshes, housing, and recreational and commercial activity along waterways. Get these maps from your county highway department, county courthouse, or the state highway department headquarters. County maps are generally very inexpensive and worth every penny.

Topographical maps (showing elevations) are also very helpful. The U.S. Geological Survey, a government agency, has mapped the entire country. Contact your state office or the national distribution office at U.S.G.S., Federal Center, Denver, CO 80225. Commercial map companies and large outdoor stores also sell topo maps. Learn to read these maps, if you don't already know how; carefully read the legend to see what various symbols mean. Spend a little time with the maps at home before heading out to the streams. Use any bits of verbal information you have been able to gather, look for tributaries of larger smallmouth rivers, look at how long the stream is and its approximate drainage area. In other words, do your homework. If you learn something about the streams beforehand, you can narrow down your list of rivers to physically investigate.

With maps and preliminary data in hand, head for the targeted streams. First check for obvious stuff – widths and depths of the stream, clarity, substrates, gradients, and adjacent land uses. Also look for signs of fishing (bait containers under bridges). Look at the waterway from several locations; you could be misled by just one observation. If the stream looks at all likely to hold fish (remember the characteristics of a good stream), get out and do some fishing. Try at least a couple of different sections.

An important way to aid your exploration is to keep records of your research. Bring a notebook along and jot down any relevant information. Trying to remember a certain bridge on a particular stream two years later is very difficult without some written notes.

More Tips on Stream Exploration

1. The best way to explore new waters is to concentrate on a single small area at a time. One or two counties is often enough. After learning that area well, move on to another section.

2. When investigating new streams, don't take just one person's word on a particular waterway. Often even nearby residents know little about these overlooked waters. Get several opinions and combine them with the information you have gathered independently.

3. In most regions, smallmouth live much farther upstream than most anglers realize. This means there are often 10 or 15 miles of overlooked headwaters even on relatively well-known rivers.

4. Many small to intermediate streams in the steep hill country of the East and Mid-South are easily wadable because of the open scoured rock and gravel bars along them. Don't refrain from fishing them just because you can't float them.

5. The smallmouth is expanding its range; in the West, more waterways are seeing bass every year. And in New England and New Brunswick the smallmouth is also expanding to new waters. Don't assume that because a waterway had no bass five or ten years ago it doesn't today.

6. Almost every major city from Kansas City to Boston has good-quality smallmouth fishing readily available. Contrast this to the poor-quality, overcrowded trout fishing available to most urban anglers, and you can see the beauty of stream smallmouth fishing.

3

Currents:
The Distinguishing Factor

ANYONE WHO HAS EVER GONE from a boat on a large lake to hip boots on a 40-foot-wide stream will quickly realize how different these types of waters are. It's important to understand the need for very different techniques on these very different waters. And even though the following methods are geared especially toward small and medium-sized streams, they can also be applied to wide, shallow rivers. Wide rocky rivers, particularly common in the eastern United States, are often only several feet deep and many smaller water approaches and techniques can be applied to them.

Three main characteristics of stream fishing make it different from other kinds of fishing. Current, of course, is one. When it comes to fishing in streams, the two things to understand about current are how well the fish are attuned to it and how to make the current work *for* you instead of against you.

The second main factor that distinguishes stream fishing is that the angler is often on foot (at least when casting). Wade fishing opens up a whole new world for the angler and also a whole new set of problems and solutions.

The third characteristic that often sets apart this type of angling is the smaller size of the "playing field." The smallness of the pools, the relative shallowness of the water, the closeness of obstacles that can impede casting, and the nearness of the target often add up to a whole new approach. In this book I'll try to show how you should specifically deal with these characteristics and use them to your advantage whenever possible.

To use current to your advantage, you must understand the basic types of current commonly encountered. It's also good to understand their causes and some effects. But you don't need an advanced course in hydrology. If you learn to recognize the few important types of currents and their causes, you will be on the road to becoming a moving-water expert. Of course, the real secret is being able to take these written descriptions and apply them to actual on-the-water situations.

CURRENT BASICS

Let's start by looking at what causes water to move in the first place—in addition to gravity, of course. The amount of fall (river gradient), the size (width and depth) of the river channel, and the amount of water flowing through the channel all determine the speed of the current. The first two—gradient and channel size—constantly change along the length of any waterway, which means current speeds are constantly changing.

This is probably the most important thing to understand about moving water: it often *changes speed and direction very quickly.* For example, in most pools, even a tiny one only 15 feet long, the water speed will vary considerably. At the head of the pool the current will be relatively fast, then at the middle (deeper) section it will slow up, and at the bottom (shallower part) of the pool it will again increase.

This changing current in a pool is a very common phenomenon, but one often not understood. And because they don't understand these different current speeds, many anglers cannot react properly to them and end up fishing the water poorly. Realizing there is a heavy current in a pool (it's easy to notice the fast, gurgling water at the head of the pool), they make a cast into that fast water. Knowing to retrieve quickly in a heavy current to keep a tight line, they really crank it back. But when the sinking lure hits the slow-moving water of midpool (where most of the fish are), it rises toward the surface and races over the best holding water. With a retrieve like that, they get few strikes. This is the most common problem the less experienced have—not reacting to the different current speeds encountered on a single retrieve. To those just starting out, the entire pool is one undifferentiated mass of moving water.

If you can intellectually realize that most of your casts will pass through different current speeds, you will possess a valuable piece of fishing knowledge. Then if you go out to the water consciously trying to detect these different speeds, after a while they will become more and more recognizable. Obviously, the main way to recognize any type of current is close visual observation. What appears at first glance to be a uniform mass of water drifting by, under careful inspection turns out to be several different currents. Anglers can also determine what the water is doing by learning how their lure reacts to different currents. In fact, a perceptive fisher knows what kind of water the lure is going through just by feel. A fast current, a slow one, a reverse flow, or an upwelling all feel different on the lure and line.

CURRENT TYPES

Now let's run through the basic types of current you will commonly encounter. These are illustrated, so I won't try to describe them in detail but just briefly discuss how fish relate to them and how to fish them.

Large Eddies

The easiest specific type of current to recognize and to fish is a large eddy or reverse flow—a side pool where the water goes in the opposite direction from the primary downstream flow. They are most often created below where a point of ground or rock bar juts out into the river channel. Many times this reverse-flowing current is very slow, nearly slack water.

The middles of these slow-moving side eddies seldom have many actively feeding bass, but they often hold inactive bass (especially if there isn't much other deep water nearby). These fish can sometimes be caught by working this slack water very diligently. In the spring, hard-bottomed eddies are favorite spawning sites for

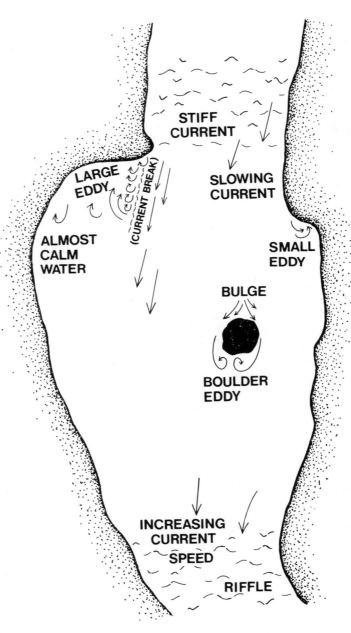

Common currents. One way to detect current behavior is to observe the movement of floating material like foam and leaves.

smallmouth. Any large eddies, even mud- or sand-bottomed ones, are good places for pickerel, pike, crappie, and sunfish. These species love still water, and in many stretches of stream the large eddies are the calmest water available.

Slower eddies are pretty easy to fish. You can work them from various positions, since the fish aren't really oriented toward any one direction. In some eddies, the water coming back upstream is moving quite fast because the downstream current is strong. In these less common fast-water eddies, it's best to fish from upstream, which will enable you to retrieve with this backward flowing water.

Current Breaks

The next type of current pattern deserving some attention is a current break, which is really just two currents coinciding. The "breaks" are especially pronounced where the current of a side pool or eddy collides with the faster-flowing main channel water. This mixing of separate currents creates a narrow strip of water, hardly more than a few inches wide, that is part turbulent and part calm. This is a favored place for smallies to position themselves. They have an easy time suspending in this zone, and lots of food is swept right to them. This type of water is hard for many to detect, and without close observation it is easy to overlook these important fish-holding areas. But once you realize where they are most likely to occur you can pinpoint them and work them carefully. This means making several casts *right through* these breaks, from a downstream position if possible.

Bulges

Another current phenomenon that should be understood by all river and creek devotees is the small "bulges" and eddies created when the current strikes large obstructions (especially rocks). There are small areas of slow-moving water both in front of and behind the obstruction. The "bulge" or slower water in front of a rock isn't very noticeable on the surface, but the small eddy of slow water behind the rock often creates a surface disturbance, a "boil." Both of these areas are worth fishing.

Many anglers will cast to the fish-holding spot downstream of the rock or log because they realize it has good potential. But most of these same people are unaware of the potential of that small niche above the rock. In fact, this position ahead of a large blunt-faced rock is where a very active bass likes to hold to be first in line for food. Even though you see little sign of this hotspot when you look at the river's surface, don't pass it up! Under most situations it's best to cast to both niches from the downstream position. Just make sure you cast far enough above the obstruction so your lure is deep enough when it passes the fish.

4 ⁓

Stream Stalking:
On-Foot Fishing

ONE OF THE MOST BASIC SKILLS of stream fishing is knowing how to approach the area that you want to fish, so that you cast properly to the waiting fish. When fishing smaller waters, the angler is often on foot, and there are two basic on-foot approaches: from downstream or from upstream.

APPROACHING FROM DOWNSTREAM

This is the classic way streams are fished on foot, especially for trout, and it is also the best approach for most stream bass fishing. The angler quietly moves into position from downstream, gets within accurate casting range of the target area, and carefully places a lure so that it will pass right by the upstream-facing fish. It isn't always possible or even desirable to use it, but this approach is the most common way of successfully working the water, and it has several advantages. For one thing, the fish are usually facing upstream into the current. So if you approach from behind (downstream of them) you can get closer without being detected. Also, because you are below the fish, any mud or debris you kick up will drift away from the fish instead of toward them. This is also partially true of the noise or vibration you cause, although a considerable amount of noise will still travel against the current to the fish.

An on-foot angler with an 18-inch smallmouth before release. The shoulder bags he uses can substitute for a fishing vest.

Cautious Approaches

It's hard to overemphasize the need for a cautious approach when wading or floating small waters. Many times over the years, I have been amazed at how easily fish in shallow or clear water can be spooked by an angler casting a shadow over the water or by noisy wading. Just as amazing is the "approach" of many anglers I've observed. They charge along the bank or wade noisily right into the pool, as if the bass could detect nothing but their lure. Learn how to wade quietly, watch your approach along the bank, and remember that if you can see a bass it can probably see you and has been put on its guard.

The fish's ability to see past the surface is largely determined by the clarity of the water. Naturally, the clearer the water the better the fish can see you. But bass can detect motion outside the water several feet away, even in water that seems extremely turbid to us. You can ease up a little closer to the fish in murky water, but still exercise plenty of caution. Remember, no matter how poor the visibility, the fish's ability to detect noise or vibrations is as good as ever.

On some streams, large schools of big carp or suckers feed in the shallow tail end of small pools and, when an angler approaches, spook wildly upstream into the pool. This near stampede of big fish into a small area is not common, but when it happens it will alarm the bass even if the bass never actually see you.

What's the solution? If you suspect a pack of big bottom feeders in the next pool, try to flush them downriver into water you have already fished. Sneak around them on the bank so you are a little upstream of them, then sort of herd them downstream. If that doesn't work and the carp or suckers alarm the smallmouth, simply sit down near the pool for five to ten minutes and let the smallies cool down. A third solution is to avoid areas that have lots of carp or suckers and move upstream to new waters.

With-the-Current Lure Retrieves

An important advantage of the downstream approach is that it allows for better lure presentation. Retrieving your lure with the current instead of against it accomplishes several things. It lets the presentation seem more natural because the lure is going the direction much of the bass's food most often travels. These food sources also travel near the bottom. This includes not only obvious bottom-dwelling creatures like crawfish and hellgrammites, but also many minnow species. Under many conditions, if your artificial bait isn't very near bottom you won't get the bass to strike. A "with-the-current" retrieve lets you do just that.

Your bait coming downstream with the current is very visible to the fish (since they're facing the current), it's moving in a natural manner, and it's down where the fish are. In strong currents it can be hard to get a lure down near the bottom and keep it there, even when you are retrieving with the current. Keeping it down when you're retrieving *against* a substantial current is nothing short of impossible. Learn to let the current *work for you* instead of against you.

A classic approach: the stream angler casts toward a visible boulder from the down-stream position.

Specific Approaches from Downstream

Let's now examine a few specific situations where you would want to approach from downstream; this includes instances where you would work from one side of the target area, casting *across and upstream*. Just remember, don't head for the rivers expecting all the spots you fish to look exactly like ones described here. Every stream, every stretch of water, indeed every pool is at least a little different from the others. The situations described here are intended to give you a general sense of how to work different categories of water.

Small Open Pools

On some streams, smallish open pools are common, especially on small pastured creeks. (Unfortunately, on more wooded or brushy streams these easy pickings aren't as common.) These situations are easy to recognize and easy to fish, compared to some others. You can stand at the bottom of the pool and easily cast to the very head of it. In a small pool of this type, the best holding water is right in the middle, which is where the fish are most of the time. Some bass move up near the riffle occasionally, but mainly in the evenings.

When fishing these pools, use plenty of stealth and caution. Get in a good casting position at the bottom of the pool, then try to avoid moving around any more. Cast your spinner, shallow-running plug, or light jig all the way to the very top of the pool and be prepared for an immediate strike. This type of strike is harder to detect than an "instant" lake strike because the current puts a belly in your line. Learn to keep the slack out of your line and *watch* your line.

If you have no immediate "take," continue the retrieve all the way through the pool, making sure you work midpool thoroughly by getting your lure deep. A tiny pool only 10 feet long and 10 feet wide is worth half a dozen casts, larger pools a few more. In some of the better waters one of these little pockets can yield over half a dozen good bass, providing you don't spook them landing other fish.

Long Narrow Pools or Glides with One Deep Side

This type of holding water is found on most of our rivers, and even though they are not the most productive places to fish

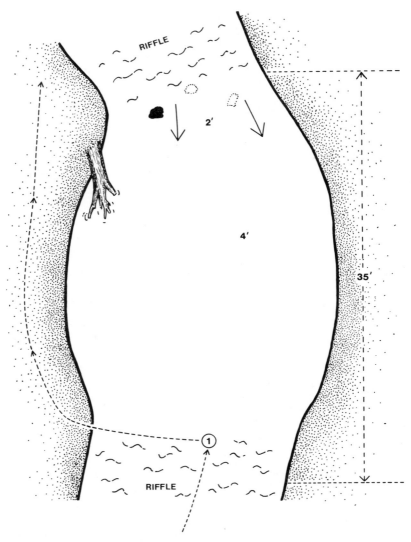

RIFFLE

2'

4'

35'

RIFFLE

①

Small pools of this type, common on many smaller waters, are easily fished from a single position. Keep wading disturbances to a minimum.

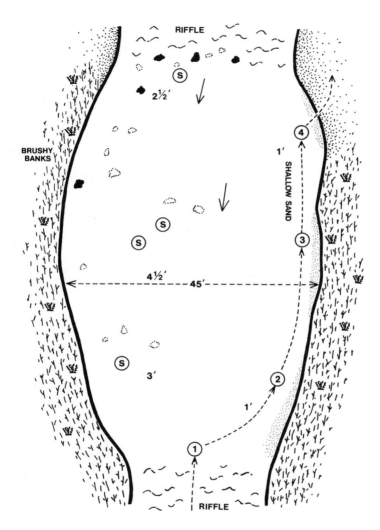

Long narrow pool with one deep side. The best way to fish a pool of this type is to move up the shallow side, through positions 1 through 4, casting across and upstream. "S" designates smallmouth.

they still merit serious attention. They can also be somewhat difficult to thoroughly cover, especially when there are roots or brush
sticking out from the deep-water bank. In this kind of spot, the fish
hang close to the bank because this is where the deepest water and
best cover are. Add a bend to the river along with those snags, and
you can see that a completely downstream approach isn't possible.

Start at position 1 in the illustration, then on to position 2,
and so on. Wade up the shallow side (very cautiously) because it has
been filled in by deposits of sand or dirt. Try to cast at an upstream
angle as much as possible because many pools or narrow glides
have considerable current, and you want to let your lure travel with
the current as much as possible. A floating diving plug sometimes
works here; a sinking lure can too often hang up if there are many
snags. Whatever you use, cast it close to that deep-water bank.
Unless the fish are in a feeding spree, they are reluctant to strike
unless your presentations are right on their doorstep.

Long Shallow Pools with Specific Targets

Some sections of streams, even ones easily large enough to
float, have little deep water. On certain rivers, large shallow areas
are created where the river flows through very rocky areas. The
channel, not able to cut down into the rock, spreads out instead.
This creates big shallow pools with many large rocks scattered in
them. In some of these, weed patches will also be present after
midsummer. But remember, the key factor determining whether a
pool of this type holds bass (and maybe pickerel or pike) is whether
it has enough big "hiding rocks"–boulders over 18 inches in diameter with at least 2 feet of water around them. This gives the
predator fish both ambush sites and places to hide when they feel
threatened. Any weeds are a short-term supplement to the rocks
and are of more interest to the pickerel or pike than to smallies.

So how do you fish waters of this type? Use the downstream
approach, realizing you are going to cast to a number of individual
targets, the "hiding rocks." Start way at the bottom and work up.
Your route upstream will be determined by the location of your
targets. Try to plan out the path *before* you start sloshing up or across
river. Even if your path is as far from fish-holding water as possible,
it's still essential to use the "wader's shuffle." Slowly and quietly
slide your feet along the bottom. Keep in mind that smallmouth

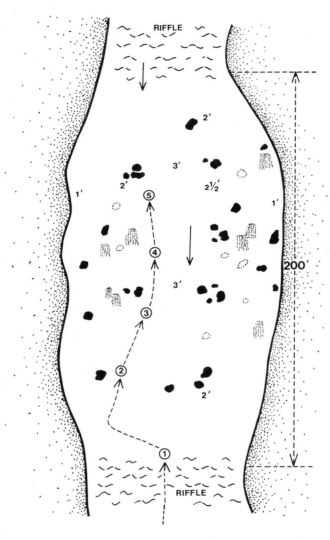

Large shallow area with visible targets. An area of this type holds fish because of the cover provided by the large boulders. Fish the rocks and weed clumps as individual targets.

under these conditions can see or hear an angler very easily. Watch your silhouette, your shadow, your wading noise, and your distance from targets. Stay as far away from them as possible, but close enough to maintain casting accuracy and hook-setting ability.

If there are weed clumps, work the small downstream pockets or eddies created by the weeds. This is where a single-hooked spinner bait comes in handy. It is unusual for these shallow flats to hold lunker smallmouth, but smaller fish can be present in good numbers. Most people, once they learn the basic techniques, really enjoy working these spots. They are also good places for a fly rodder who wants lots of open targets and room for backcasts.

Undercut Banks with No Snags

Experienced small-creek trout anglers know the potential of these little hidden hotspots. Those in pursuit of creek bass should be aware that undercuts also hold their quarry. First you have to recognize fish-holding undercuts, then figure out how to fish them. An undercut is a stream bank that has been undermined (washed out) below the surface by the force of the current. It most commonly occurs on the outside bend of streams with low soil banks (not rocky ones) with a thick root system that keeps the above-water portion of the bank from collapsing. Trout will use the smallest of undercuts; bass like slightly bigger ones. Pike, pickerel, catfish, and walleye also like to lie in them if they are big enough. The best way to discover the size or kinds of undercuts that have fish is to start fishing all kinds of them until you find the types that produce.

However, fishing these underground hangouts can be a little tricky. Smallmouth, unless very active, won't come very far out of their lair for your lure, so you have to go in after them. Approach from downstream and the opposite side of the creek. It's very important to get as close to the undercut as possible so that your cast will be as short as possible. To get the lure under the bank and maintain line control, the rod-to-lure distance has to be short. Spinners can often be manipulated so that the current washes them under the bank and downstream. It takes some experimenting to be able to feel when you're getting under the bank and also keeping enough line tension, so try spinners of different weights until you discover the best one. If snags (like tree roots) are present, this way of working cutbanks isn't very good. The next section discussing some upstream approaches will deal with undercuts with snags.

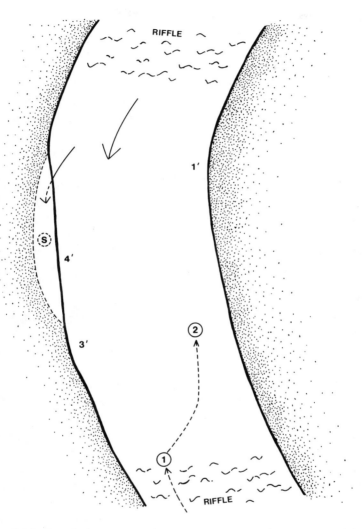

Undercut bank. From both positions, it's important to get your lure upstream of the undercut so that when you retrieve it the current will pull it under the bank.

Large Pools Too Deep to Wade

Even on some of the smaller waters, you will find pools too deep or otherwise impractical to fish by standing in the water. Larger rivers will probably have many pools of this type. Faced with a large pool (too long to cast from bottom to top), wise anglers plan their approach with care, looking at the pool *before* fishing it and deciding the most favorable areas of the pool to fish and the best places to fish from.

You can begin by fishing the very bottom section of the pool by the classic method – wading up from the downriver shallows and thoroughly covering this portion. These tail sections of deep water are sometimes good for bass. But before you go too far, do some visual scouting. Even though both banks are pretty low and open (no trees or brush), you may realize one side of the pool is rockier than the other. Quietly move to this bank, where the water is both a little deeper and much rockier. Since the pool is too wide to cast across, focus your attention on the better-looking side. From the bank you still use the "cast up and bring it back with the current" technique. Well, not quite – being on the bank, you will have to make quartering casts, *up and across stream*.

The two biggest problems with this approach are being seen by the fish and not getting the presentation down deep enough. Both problems are caused by the same factor: too much height. Even if the riverbank you are on is only a few feet high, it still puts you (and your rod) at least 7 to 8 feet above the water. If the water clarity is at all good, wary smallmouth will easily spot your towering frame as you move along the bank high above them. Worse, even if some of the deeper fish don't detect you, your lure probably won't reach them. Since you're not able to cast directly upstream and are at a relatively sharp angle to the pool bottom, that belly in your line and sharp angle will keep your lure running shallow. The solution is obvious: *get lower,* both you and your rod. Moving along the shore in a "low crouch" position can lessen the risk of spooking the fish. When you stop and start casting, do it on your knees; you'll get the rod tip at a better angle to the water.

A final note: looking at the illustration, you see the angler crossing the river at the upstream riffle and fishing the shallower eddy on the opposite side. This is because these waters hold pickerel or pike, and the large log in the calm eddy would be a likely spot for

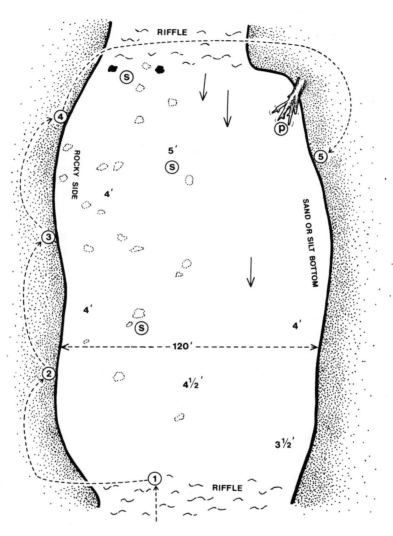

Large pool too deep to wade with clear water. Positions 2 through 5 should be approached in a crouch and fished kneeling. The log near position 5 is productive only if pickerel or pike are present.

these fish. If the log wasn't there or there were no pike or pickerel in this stream, a knowledgeable angler would skip the shallow sandy side altogether and head directly upstream to new waters.

Riprapped Banks

Riprapped banks (where rocks, pieces of concrete, bricks, or other hard material have been placed along riverbanks to prevent bank erosion) are good fish producers, easy to identify, and not too difficult to fish. Some large rivers that see heavy boat or commercial barge traffic have had many miles of banks riprapped. Smaller waterways seldom see this much bank protection. On most bass streams only relatively short portions of banks are riprapped. These are generally around bridges, where roadways pass near rivers, and where towns or commercial enterprises have been built on riverbanks. Riprap is also found in agricultural areas. Farmers will dump the rock they collect off their fields into nearby streams. Sometimes they do this to stop bank erosion; other times it's simply a way to get rid of field rock. On some streams that have been heavily silted in by intensive streamside farming, "ag rock" riprap has become a major source of remaining rocky substrate. On these streams, nearly every bank that has been riprapped in this way will hold smallmouth, since so much natural rocky habitat has been lost.

Even rivers with plenty of natural rock remaining see lots of smallmouth around riprap. This is because the great number of crevices and crannies created by riprapping makes for many hiding places for crawfish, minnows, and other bass food. During peak feeding periods of the year, riprap areas are consistently productive. Some riprap areas even attract bass during the spawn period. If the riprap has some boulder-sized rock in it, the fish will seek out the little pockets created by these big rocks for spawning sites.

If a stream is narrow enough, the on-foot angler can fish a riprap area from the opposite bank. Approaching from the opposite side of the stream, the angler can make quartering (45-degree) casts across and upstream. Thoroughly work the riprap; make several casts from a position, then move forward 15 or 20 feet and repeat the process until you are at the upstream end of the riprap. A shallow-running float-diving crankbait is deadly and doesn't hang up too much. If the current along the riprap isn't too stiff, topwater lures dropped right along the bank are also productive.

For rivers too wide to cast across, fishing from the riprapped side is possible. Using an in-line spinner or a spinner bait, first cast parallel to the bank and bring the bait back within a couple feet of the water's edge. Next cast 4 or 5 feet from shore and let the lure sink so the deeper water can be covered. The casts close to shore will get the very active bank-facing fish and the deeper casts should tempt the deeper-holding ones. Extra walking or wading caution is advised; the slippery (and sometimes loose) rocks used for riprap can be a little tricky to walk on.

APPROACHING FROM UPSTREAM

Faced with certain conditions, a moving-water fisher should switch to the other basic on-foot technique: approaching the target from upstream and working the lure against the current. If you fish even a fair amount of diverse waters during a season, you will have to use this technique.

As a general rule, when you're working your way upriver on foot and you must go to an upstream position to cast, *skirt the fish-holding water*–that is, stay a safe distance away from the water you intend to fish. Notice some of the illustrations for examples of this. Too many eager, inexperienced fishers charge right along the edge of the bank to get to their casting spot. If the water is clear, their fishing is ruined before it gets started. Take the extra few seconds to get in position *without* disturbing the fish.

Undercut Banks with Snag

Here we have a fishy-looking undercut with one big problem: a very obvious root system protruding into the undercut from a small tree growing on the bank. Worse yet, some large branches have washed down and tangled in the roots, making a thorough fishing of the undercut from downstream impossible. After working the lower end of the undercut, sneak around to the upstream position and ease in as close as possible (making sure no mud is washed into the fishing zone). Study the current carefully and determine from what position your casts will be carried under the bank–somewhere above and across from the undercut. You are going to attempt to get your presentation to wash under the bank

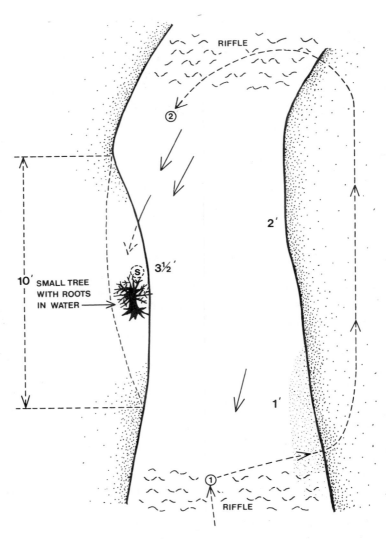

Undercut with snag. From position 1 you have difficulty getting your lure under the bank without snagging. From position 2 you can use the current to pull your lure under the bank.

(at least a little) and downstream, settle toward the bottom, and be stopped *before* it hangs up in the snag.

If you are unwilling to risk losing lures, this is not the place for you to be fishing. Casting up near snags of this sort is risky but not impossible. A weed-guard–equipped, single-hooked spinner will lessen the snagging risk. A slow-sinking type that spins very easily is the one you want.

When you believe the lure is near the snag, stop its downstream movement and let it start being pulled out from under the bank to a position directly below you in midcurrent. Keep working your bait like this for several casts if the cutbank seems like a good one. At times it takes a good number of casts to either present the bait just right or tease the fish into striking. Of course, if you hook a very strong fish like a larger bass or pike, you will have to horse it quickly away from the roots.

Pools with Large Obstructions

Here is a sad situation that confronts the angler from time to time. You come around the bend and find a fine-looking small pool, but filling up most of it is a big snag. Most of the "open" water is a section between the pool head and the obstruction. Even though this blocked pool presents some problems, it's still probably easier to fish than the undercut with a snag.

The stalk to get into a good position is critical. Some fish may be close to the riffle in shallow water, so make your first cast a good distance away from the head of the pool. Careful wading in a hard-bottomed riffle (rock, gravel, clean sand) shouldn't send too much debris down to the fish. But if the stream bottom is very soft, especially with mud, don't wade out into the channel; try to work the water from near the bank instead.

After catching any top-of-the-pool bass, you should sneak a little closer to the snag. Crouch down to shave a couple of feet off your silhouette. Often, when the riffle is shallow I actually kneel down in the water so I'm less visible. The intent is to get close enough to the obstruction so you will have very good lure control. In moderate current, try to keep your lure stationary as close as possible to the snag. Many plugs designed to be retrieved slowly will do the job, including the Flatfish. Some spinners will also work; lightweight ones that spin very easily are best. If you put

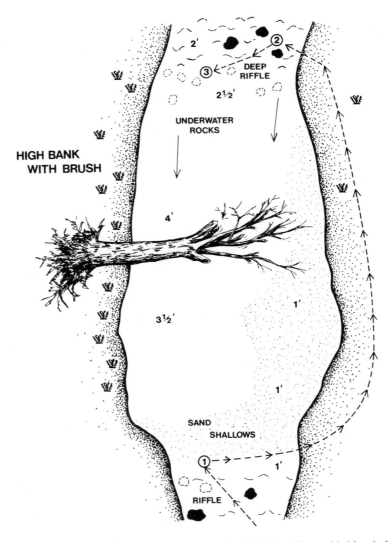

Pool with a large obstruction. Position 2 is used to fish the boulder-studded head of the pool. After working the head-of-pool area, move to position 3 to fish down toward the blocking tree.

some lead 14 inches or so ahead of the spinner, it will go down but still ride a little off the bottom. Using this "hold it in front of their noses" method, you can draw at least a few fish out from the snag.

Deep Riffles with Large Rocks

This method of holding your lure steady in the current is also good in a deep riffle or glide with large rocks, a place where rocks (or less often, wood) hold bass but the current is strong. (A glide is a narrow pool with moderate current throughout.) You want to put the bait into as many likely fish-holding spots as possible. If you cast from directly downstream, your bait is swept away from the fish too quickly. But with an upstream or up-and-across-stream approach, your presentation stays in front of the fish longer and on a tight line.

The fly fisher can work a fly through each small pocket in a few seconds. The spin fisher has to crank the lure all the way back, of course, before casting to another spot. With either type of tackle, evenings are generally the best times. In fact, if a riffle or glide of this type is adjoining deeper holding water, the last couple of hours of daylight can see many smallmouth moving into the rocky shallows.

"Body Fishing"

In this unusual approach, the idea is to wade out into the river, create a small eddy with your body, and then fish in that eddy. I'm not kidding—body fishing really is practiced on some rivers. It works best in large pools or glides with moderate current flows and depths and somewhat low water clarity. Midsummer to late summer is the best time to try it.

From upstream, wade slowly and quietly down into the upper end of a large pool, where the water is 3 to 4 feet deep. When the water is around waist deep, stop moving. If the current is moderate (not too slow), a fair-sized swirling eddy will be created right in front of you. (Don't try this in very strong current where you might lose your footing.) After five to ten minutes some bass will swim right into the eddy in front of you. By working a jig or spinner right in front of you, you can catch several bass from this single spot. Then move to another (similar) location in this pool and repeat the process.

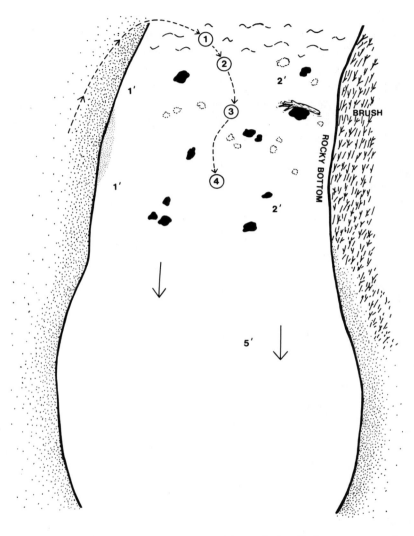

Wade fishing a deep riffle with a stiff current. Smallmouth will often move into a deep riffle or glide to feed. Strong current makes fly or lure control difficult from downstream. Be careful not to create a mud plume from the upstream position.

What makes body fishing work? During the peak of summer feeding activity, bass in *large* pools move around a fair amount looking for food. This is particularly true of smaller fish, which are quite numerous and don't have the best feeding/holding sites to start with. As these fish move around, they detect protection from the current (your eddy) and swim into it. The body fishing technique seems to work best on a gravel or pebble bottom, possibly because your feet stir up this bottom material and make the fish think food sources are being dislodged. Body fishing rarely works in water that has good visibility. If you can see your feet, the water is too clear for body fishing. It also doesn't work in small waters, where wading into the fish's environment invariably alarms them.

5

Float Fishing
for Smallmouth

I LOVE RIVER FLOATING; I love to sit back and let the current do much of the work as I quietly pass new sights with the rounding of every bend. In many situations, using a canoe, johnboat, or other small craft is not only a fine way to see a river, but also the most productive way to fish it. Of course float fishing does have limitations. Many streams or sections of streams simply cannot be floated; only on-foot anglers can pursue their fish. Float fishing also takes a little more equipment and organizing effort than just heading up the stream in your hip boots. But if you learn where and how to use watercraft, float fishing can add greatly to your stream-fishing enjoyment.

Floatable moving waters can be divided into two types: easy and difficult. Easy rivers can be floated by almost anyone using almost any type of canoe or light johnboat. This includes almost all large and many intermediate-sized flat (that is, without whitewater) rivers. Many of these waters are easy to float but difficult to cover thoroughly on foot. Fortunately for the smallmouth angler, there are still many of these streams across the fish's range. Word of mouth and state or regional canoe guides will steer you to many of them.

The second type of streams are difficult to fish on foot and also challenging to float. Because of downed trees, narrowness of the channel, or shallow riffles, they require modification in standard floating techniques and greater skill. But with proper planning and equipment, experienced float fishers can enjoy these waters, too.

FLOAT FISHING BASICS

Safety and Preparation

Safety should be a consideration in any floating activity. Fortunately, most bass streams are not particularly hazardous and do not require a great deal of boat-handling skill. However, you should at least be familiar with the basics of water safety and handling your craft before heading out. If you need help, a number of books on canoeing and boating discuss safety and handling techniques. Canoeing clubs offer classes, and knowledgeable friends or acquaintances are also good sources of advice.

The main kind of preparation you may need is learning what kind of conditions to expect. Don't start your first float trip on a difficult river. Find out whether you may need to lift or drag your

Bank shooting, as these two eastern anglers are doing from a johnboat, can be a productive technique for all species of black bass.

craft through shallow riffles or maneuver around trees blocking the stream, and plan your gear accordingly. Know your stream before you go, and a float down one of our continent's varied waterways will be an exciting and productive adventure.

One more note on preparing for your trip: float fishing should not be confused with simply floating a river. When you decide to fish a stream by floating, make sure your trip partners also have the same goals.

Common Float-Fishing Mistakes

Here is an all-too-common scenario: Anglers X and Y drift merrily down the stream, randomly flinging casts as they go. Halfway through their 14-mile float, they realize it's late in the day and they haven't caught many fish. They hurriedly paddle or row the last few miles, disappointed that the river has such poor fishing. What did they do wrong (assuming the river does have fish in it)? Probably several things.

For one, they floated entirely too much water. Rivers that have even moderate amounts of fish-holding water per mile should be floated in increments of only several miles per trip. Rivers with only widely scattered good water are another matter, but here we are talking about the more common rivers with at least three or four fish-holding stretches per mile. So first plan a realistic float distance: 5 or 6 miles is much more appropriate than 13 or 14, where you end up floating a lot more than fishing.

Another mistake was that they both tried to fish simultaneously and so their craft was out of control, drifting this way and that. Take turns fishing and controlling your craft. Both of you will catch more fish if one person carefully positions the canoe for proper lure presentation *and maintains* that position. Our friends also let their craft spook the fish. Be careful not to drift too close to the fish, bang and splash, or cast shadows over the fish.

The final major mistake was not being selective and disciplined in their fishing. Fishing anywhere and everywhere for several hours, they found themselves miles from the landing with little time left. They wasted hundreds of casts on unproductive water, then passed over good areas in a hurry. Pace yourself; cover the good water thoroughly but quickly pass over the poor water.

Your Game Plan

The ill-fated trip described above should point to a need for an overall game plan for your float. First, select a reasonable float distance; don't bite off more than you can fish and paddle. Know the river levels beforehand, not only for fishing success, but also so you can determine your travel time. (For instance, the moderate water levels and flow rates of May are often very different from the slow flows and low waters of August.) On a stream with a slow to moderate current, travel speed is about 2 to 3 miles per hour—and that does not factor in fishing time. If you plan on being off the river before dark—which is generally an excellent idea—check your time at various points to see that you are not falling behind schedule.

Also know the type of water you will be paddling over, or at least prepare for the unexpected. For instance, if the river has lots of shallow boulder fields where you must get out and drag your canoe, your trip will take far longer than expected. And if it's a cool day, you'll be sorry if you didn't bring hip boots.

Be sure to consider vehicle parking at put-in and take-out points and the quality of connecting roadways. Don't head out to a river without good maps and information on roadways and access points. Good canoe guides or stream guides are invaluable sources for this.

FISHING TECHNIQUES FROM CANOES OR JOHNBOATS

Bank Shooting

The most popular way of fishing from a stream craft is using a controlled drift to make carefully targeted casts to the banks. This "bank shooting," as it is often called, is effective on many river stretches that are over 50 feet wide. The idea is to thoroughly fish the holding water along the banks of pools or glides. This would include logs, brush, rocks, undercuts, and vegetation in water deep

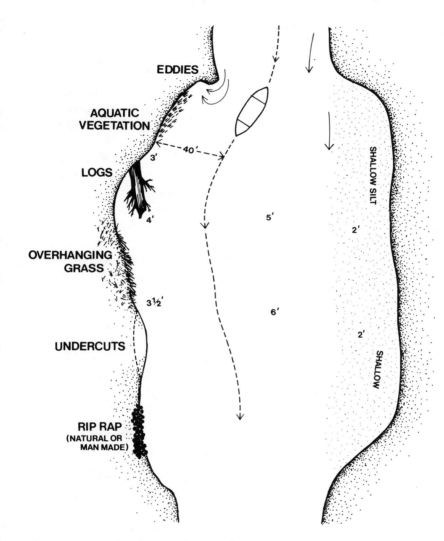

Casting to typical bank targets. The craft must be controlled to maintain proper distance and speed.

enough to hold fish – at least 18 inches. Riprap banks are very good targets for bank shooting if the current isn't too strong.

The canoe must be kept the proper distance from the bank and the speed of the drift must be slowed to enable sufficient casts. (I specifically describe how this kind of fishing is done from a canoe, since canoes are the most popular stream craft. However, the basic techniques and principles also apply to other small watercraft.) Don't get too close to the bank you are fishing – 35 feet is near enough. The person in the stern must position the canoe while the other fishes. Switch roles every twenty minutes, every other pool, or whatever you jointly agree on. If the person in the bow turns around and sits facing the stern, you can easily switch often. The fly rod really shines with this method. You can deliver accurate casts quickly and easily to every fishy-looking spot.

Both anglers can bank shoot at the same time by employing a boat drag – a heavy chain, 3 or 4 feet long, on the end of a rope behind the craft. With it you can slow down the boat so that both people can fish. This method won't work everywhere, since currents don't always cooperate and over soft bottoms a mud cloud will be generated, but in some situations it's a good way to increase your fishing time. One word of caution: never tie a drag to the *side* of your craft, especially a canoe. If the drag catches bottom in strong current, it can pull the canoe over or swamp it.

"Sneak Technique"

A good method to fish many pools and banks on rivers of lesser size is what I call the "sneak technique." The idea is to sneak close along one side of the stream channel so you won't spook the fish. Choose the side of the pool that is shallowest or farthest away from the area you will fish. Quietly move into position so that you can cast upstream and across the pool. The canoe can also be controlled easily from this position. In shallow and slow-moving water, the canoe handler can stay in place by sticking a paddle into the bottom. If you approach a pool that you're not sure is deep enough to hold fish, be cautious and sneak. If it turns out to be shallow, fishless water, no harm is done. But if the pool looks good as you edge around it, you will be in a position to take advantage of it.

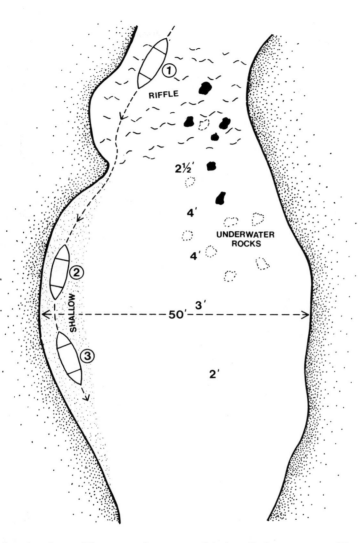

The "sneak technique." Position 1 allows you to fish the riffle from upstream. Then you can sneak into positions 2 and 3 and work the pool by casting across and upstream.

Vertical Jigging

Vertical jigging (fishing directly below your craft) is normally done on lakes or deep rivers, rather than on shallow rivers. However, this technique does come in handy for stream fishing in some instances. River areas with lots of large logs or whole trees sunk in deep water are hard to fish with conventional techniques. But if you quietly drift down to the tree and tie up to its above-water branches, you can get right above the fish. The water around the wood cover should be at least 4 or 5 feet deep and the clarity of the water should be low. Don't try this method in shallower water or where the water is very clear; you'll only spook the fish. Moderately turbid rivers of at least intermediate size, where the current washes out deep "holes" around large logs or stumps, are the best place to fish vertically.

Use jigs just heavy enough to get to the bottom. Slowly "swim" the jig with the current, right along the bottom. Use scent on the jig or, better yet, tip it with a piece of bait. Because the fish have plenty of time to smell the slow-moving lure, you'll get a lot of strikes. If the underwater cover has lots of limbs or roots, you'll need a weed-guard–equipped jig. A long rod allows you to manipulate your bait much better than a short one unless you are fishing right under the craft. Strikes with this method may be extremely light; watch closely for the slightest unusual movement of the line and instantly set the hook. And remember, be quiet! Any banging on your craft will shut the fish down.

Anchoring–Why, How, and Where

An anchor is essential whenever the current or wind is too strong for you to maintain your position while fishing from a craft–for example, a riprap bank where the current is too strong for thorough bank shooting. Anchoring at a 45-degree angle (across and downstream) from the riprap you intend to fish is the best alternative. You'll also need an anchor when you plan to fish from the same place for an extended period. (See illustration for other examples.)

Situations where anchoring is needed come up with significant regularity on most floats. So don't head down the river without a good anchor (or even better, two anchors, for both bow and stern). Get a fairly heavy one for the stern so you can use a short anchor rope and still stay put. Remember, use the anchors to put yourself in a good casting position—either above, below, or across from the fish. Don't anchor so close to the fish or create so much ruckus that you spook your quarry. You'll need an easy-to-use (and quiet) anchor system. Move quietly into position, anticipating the amount of drift in the current and calculating where the craft will be when it finally comes to a halt.

One specific place where anchoring pays off is upstream of a downed tree that is substantially or wholly blocking the channel of a smaller river. If the water is at least 3 feet deep, various species use these areas as feeding or holding spots. Unfortunately, these places are seldom easy to fish, but with careful canoe positioning and snagless baits it can be done. If the water visibility is high, make sure you stay far enough upstream to avoid alarming the fish—at least 25 feet. Also be careful that your anchor dragging on the bottom doesn't send a lot of mud down into the log jam.

Another good place to anchor is in a long pool that is shallow or silty on one side and has too much current for you to stay in position otherwise. Especially when the fish are inactive, anchoring on the fishless side and working the fish-holding part of the pool from top to bottom can be successful. Anchoring both bow and stern really helps here. With only one anchor, the craft will swing from side to side in the multiple currents, making it difficult to detect strikes.

DIFFICULT-TO-FLOAT WATERS

There are smallmouth streams in most regions that require considerable effort to float, but with the right equipment and good preparation even these can provide very satisfying and productive trips. I have found over forty of these "challenging" streams in the upper Midwest alone, including over twenty that have enough very shallow summertime riffles to keep the average canoeist off them. Add at least another twenty that are off limits because of downed trees, and you have over one thousand miles of stream in just this one region that rarely see a float fisher and only occasionally an on-foot angler. Their mostly untapped fisheries are waiting for you to take

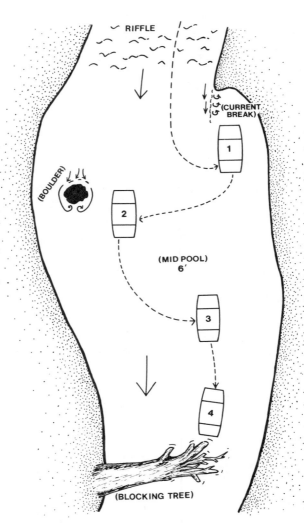

Fishing from an anchored craft. Boat position 1 is the best place from which to fish the current break. Position 2 is for the boulder, position 3 for the midpool area, and position 4 for the tree. Note that the boat path avoids getting too close to fishing targets.

up the challenge. Many of these waters or adjacent lands also provide excellent duck and squirrel hunting, camping, bird watching,
and all-around "get away from it all" day trips.

Other regions of the country where smallmouth are native
(or where they have been widely introduced, like the eastern sea-
board river systems) also have these seldom-floated streams. Even
heavily populated Ohio and Indiana still have numerous overlooked
floatable waterways. Trees blocking the stream channel will be the
main difficulty. The Missouri and Arkansas Ozarks and the river
smallmouth areas of Kentucky still have many small waters not yet
destroyed by dams. These streams suffer from shallow riffles during
summer low flows, but can be navigated with a little extra work,
especially when water levels are slightly above normal.

It should be understood that I'm *not* discussing whitewater
rivers in this category of difficult waters. Whitewater (especially in
the eastern mountain regions) generally can be safely floated only
in decked boats (covered kayaks or canoes) or large rafts. Fishing
under these conditions isn't easy. Besides, many whitewater rivers
are too cold or have currents too strong to produce good populations
of bass. The difficult waters I'm referring to here are the kind
blocked by trees or shallow riffles, and perhaps occasional rapids.

Equipment and Techniques

For streams of this type a very light craft—one that can be easily
lifted around trees or pulled through shallow riffles—is almost essential. Standard-weight boats (75 pounds or more) do not work well.
Your fishing gear and other equipment must also be kept light, and
must be packed so it can be easily carried. Expect to bring plenty of
water into the canoe as you jump in and out; if you carry anything
that must stay dry, keep it in a waterproof container. Floating distances should also be kept short. On streams where travel speed is
particularly slow, 3 or 4 miles is enough. Allow extra time so that
you don't get caught on the stream after dark.

Actual fishing techniques on tough streams will, of course,
vary widely. You may use everything from "park-and-wade"
fishing, to bank shooting, to anchoring to fish. On streams with
numerous trees blocking the channel, anchoring above these ob-

structions (or vertical jigging if the water is deep enough) will be very useful.

Another category of difficult rivers not commonly floated by bass anglers are those with only widely scattered good water. These rivers have high amounts of unproductive sandy or gravel substrate or shallow stretches and only small amounts of rocky substrate in deeper water. They often have good fishing in these few and far-between spots, but are almost impossible to cover on foot. The secret to success lies in targeting the fishing areas and in travel discipline.

If these waterways are deep enough to allow the use of a small motor, travel between good spots will be considerably quicker and easier. Unfortunately for those who desire motorized travel, even the smallest of motors don't always work on extra-shallow, sandy rivers. Learn where the good areas are, so you can concentrate on them and travel from one to another without wasting time. Even five or six fish-producing spots in a long 8 or 9 miles of river can give you a fair day's fishing. Just plan on exercising your paddling arm as well as your casting arm.

THE CRAFT AS TRANSPORTATION ONLY

On some streams – or sections of streams – your craft should be used only to move you down the river, *not* as a fishing platform. Many intermediate-sized waters (say 25 to 50 feet wide) are large enough to float, but are too narrow or shallow to cast from the craft without scaring the fish. Common sense should tell you that drifting through the middle of a pool 30 feet wide and 3 feet deep in your 17-foot Old Town and casting to the fish at the same time is the wrong way to go. But I've seen plenty of guys banging their way down a small, shallow waterway and floating right over the fish while they cast around them.

An example may illustrate this point better. I know a couple of smallmouth anglers in the Missouri Ozarks who have been floating and fishing the many fine streams in their region for nearly forty years. Years ago, when their local streams were filled with uneducated, eager bass, anyone on a leisurely float down a local stream was almost guaranteed to get plenty of fish. Sloppy technique didn't matter too much; even if they scared some bass there were always plenty more. Nowadays it's a different story. With increased pressure, there are fewer and smarter bass. Unfortunately, these two veteran anglers haven't updated their floating techniques. They still drift right over the fish and both try to fish at once. They rarely anchor and infrequently get out to wade, even where on-foot fishing is obviously called for. The result–they catch a lot less bass than they used to. Their tackle may be modern, but their floating techniques are still 1940.

These anglers and thousands of others like them could easily improve their catch rate by improving their floating methods. This type of sloppy fishing comes from lack of understanding (and probably a little laziness, too). Fish in small, *shallow,* and *clear* water (especially bass) are often disturbed by a watercraft passing too close or by its shadow, and will not feed for several minutes–the minutes you're casting to them. Laziness is another matter. It *is* easier to let the craft drift along willy-nilly rather than control its drift, and easier to throw casts while sitting than to get out and sneak up to the fish on foot. Prepare to put a little effort into float fishing. It's especially crucial to realize you will need to get out of the craft regularly–unless you just want to take a leisurely float instead of catching fish!

But when to get out? You need to know *before* you float through a small pool and spook the fish that it is fish-holding water. The best way to do this is for both anglers to keep a sharp eye on the water ahead and quickly stop if the water looks even possible. Stop at least several yards above the head of the pool or glide. Then cautiously approach the spot (probably from the bank) and decide if it's worth fishing. If not, all you lost was a few moments of time. If the water does look worth a try, simply fish it with the approach that is appropriate for the situation. This may mean sneaking along the bank (away from the water) down to the bottom of the pool. An alternative is to float right through the pool. The fish will probably be spooked, but if you are willing to wait five or ten minutes and then start fishing, many of the fish will be calmed down enough to catch.

ONE-PERSON FLOATING

If you can't round up a partner when you want to float the river, try going alone. Plan on anchoring or parking your canoe often and fishing on foot, since controlling the canoe and casting at the same time is tough. But otherwise, solo float trips aren't difficult.

The first thing you will need is a craft you can easily handle by yourself (loading, launching, portaging, and paddling). Several types of small, light watercraft work especially well as solo craft. Short (13-foot), solid solo canoes, super-lightweight (Kevlar) standard-length models, and lightweight inflatable canoes do the job. If you can load a standard-weight canoe by yourself and stick to easy streams, even your regular canoe will work. And of course, larger waterways with drive-down trailer landings allow one-person johnboat floats. Perhaps the most unusual possibility for solo trips is a float tube. These updated inner tubes (often called belly boats) are still a rarity on smallmouth streams, but can be used very effectively on certain waters. All the one-person crafts I've mentioned

A lone angler easily carries his lightweight inflatable canoe and gear around an obstruction on a narrow, heavily wooded waterway.

Two float fishers use the one-vehicle method by substituting a bicycle for the second car.

are under 40 pounds in weight. For example, I use an 11½-foot, 30-pound inflatable canoe that can be easily carried on one shoulder while I carry a rod and paddle with my other hand. This rugged little craft isn't the best boat to fish out of, since you sit so low in the water, but one or two anglers can use it to transport themselves down very small streams. And these inflatables cost less than $200.

An extra word about float tubes. They are especially effective for fishing short distances on mountain streams with very steep banks. Some small Allegheny and Ozark mountain creeks have long, deep pools, nearly impossible to traverse on foot, separated by long, shallow riffles. Using a canoe on these unusual streams means lots of getting out and dragging. With the belly boat you can easily walk through the riffles with your "boat" attached, but still float (using fins on your feet) through the deep areas. A mile or two of stream is enough to cover with this method.

Float trips are usually done with two vehicles to shuttle back and forth between put-in and take-out. But a solo angler can do a one-vehicle float trip. To do this you'll need a motor vehicle that will carry the watercraft, a bicycle or a small motorized two-wheeler (like a moped), and your fishing gear. Even small station wagons or hatchbacks do fine with a canoe and bike combo. Just drop your bike or moped off at the bottom of the float route (out of sight, chained to a tree) and drive up to your launch site. At the end of your float, simply bike back to get your car and load up your gear. It's a good idea to keep your float distances a little shorter than normal.

This one-vehicle float method is a good option even when fishing or canoeing with a partner; it allows you to ride together and saves vehicle wear and cost.

If you have trouble getting a bike into your car, there are handy bike racks available. Some easily attach to hatchback or station wagon doors and can be removed in seconds. Others attach to the car's bumper. An outside rack is particularly good for gasoline-powered mopeds or motor bikes, because the rack allows you to carry them upright and outside the car.

FLOATING HEAVILY USED WATERS

Heavily used streams are still a distinct minority, but some rivers are becoming more popular every day. If streams you want to fish are heavily used by other float fishers, there are several things you can do to either beat the crowds or catch fish that others have missed.

To avoid other float fishers (or pleasure canoeists), go on a weekday instead of the weekend, or schedule your trips before Memorial Day or after Labor Day. If you do float on the weekend during the summer, you can often get a jump on other floaters with an early-morning start. If you can leave the launch site an hour or more before the others, you will probably stay ahead of them all day. Commercial canoe rentals seldom launch many canoes before 9:00 A.M., so a 6:00 or 7:00 A.M. start lets you put some miles between you and the rental crowd.

Actually catching fish on heavily fished float rivers can be a real challenge, especially as the season wears on. The bass that survive the onslaught of anglers casting to them day after day become wary critters. A smart fisher will seek out the overlooked spots – eddies or pockets next to a fast riffle, little side channels no one floats down, any place average floaters would miss because they are drifting past too fast, or where they can't fish because they won't get out of their craft. If you take the time to work these little overlooked places you will likely find good bass.

The final way to beat the crowd is to stay completely off the heavily floated sections of popular rivers. You don't need to stay off these waterways altogether; just concentrate on the many miles of good water *above* the sections that are commonly floated. These upper reaches may be too small for easy floating, but are often still passable with a little extra effort. And don't assume that because this part of the stream isn't huge it can't have any good fishing. I've seen plenty of outstanding 3-pound bronzebacks come from these upper waters.

SAME-SITE FLOATING

Same-site floating means that you return to the same launch site after floating. This method has its limitations and certainly can't be used everywhere, but it also has some advantages. For one thing, you eliminate the logistics hassle of extra vehicles or bicycling. Just launch the craft, work your way upstream for a couple of miles, and then float back. This method of floating also has the advantage of forcing you to fish more slowly and more thoroughly, since the amount of stream you can cover is so limited.

Obviously, this method is meant for water with only mild current. Streams with long pools interspersed with short riffles do fine. It makes especially good sense where extremely steep or brushy banks make on-foot travel difficult. Use a light craft and moderate amounts of gear to make the upstream paddle easier.

If you are willing to pull some extra weight, you can also use this method for camping. Using a canoe to transport your camping gear a mile or so upstream (or down), you can access many fine streamside campsites.

FLOAT-FISHING EQUIPMENT

It's important to get the right equipment for your float fishing. But that doesn't necessarily mean expensive gear. The necessary items for enjoyable float fishing can be very reasonable, especially compared to all those high-ticket items so common to lake angling.

Watercraft

A canoe of some type is best for the smaller floatable waters; a small johnboat is better for the bigger waters. A light, 12-foot or 14-foot "john" equipped with oars or paddles and maybe a small motor will work fine if little lifting, dragging, or narrow passages are encountered. Johnboats have the advantage of being very stable craft. They are much easier to fish out of than canoes and allow the angler to stand up and move around. They are also very difficult to capsize and allow you to easily carry huge quantities of gear. But to obtain these advantages you must have waterways big enough to float the johnboat. This rules out rivers with lots of shallow riffles, extremely narrow passages, or trees blocking the channel. You must be willing to deal with a significantly heavier craft and have adequate launching and landing sites. Rough landings—down steep embankments or through brush—while no great challenge to the canoeist, are very tough for the johnboat user. Johnboats are also harder to transport. Few can be put on and off (or in) a motor vehicle or trailer as easily as a canoe.

Lightweight canoes, however, will perform on almost any type of floatable stream, large or small. And they are so lightweight they can even be loaded and unloaded by one person. If you can't afford a new craft, look for a used one. Your choice should be a light (under 70 pounds), nonaluminum model with no keel or a low (whitewater) keel. Aluminum, while acceptable, has a tendency to grab on rocks instead of sliding off. Whitewater models with no keels slip from side to side much better than standard "lake" models with keels.

Motors

What about a motor on your craft? For small and intermediate waterways, motors have only very limited potential and I don't think they are worth the bother. A few smaller "mountain" rivers might be an exception to this rule; they have slow and deep pools several hundred yards long, separated by short fast rapids or riffles. In these situations a small motor can be helpful, as long as you are careful about lifting the prop out of the water *before* reaching the riffles. For larger, deeper rivers, motors can also be used successfully, especially during the higher river levels of spring and early summer.

Unless the river you are going to fish is unusually deep and also free of rocks and logs, don't use a large motor. Too often, lake anglers try to use their large powerful motors on rivers – with bad results. Hitting just one large rock at high speed can seriously damage your rig (and yourself).

A smaller motor of only 5 horsepower or a little more is enough to push your johnboat along nicely, and keeps you moving slow enough to see and avoid obstacles. Canoe owners often make the opposite mistake about motor size – they choose one too light to do the job. Electric trolling motors should develop at least 28 pounds of thrust. A 2 horsepower gas motor, while noisier and dirtier, will really push a canoe along also.

Miscellaneous Gear

Finally, we should consider a few odds and ends needed for floating. Paddles are largely a matter of personal choice; I prefer inexpensive wooden ones that I don't worry about breaking. A waterproof bag or container is handy for extra clothes, camera, and maps or books – not so much for spills but protection from the water on the bottom of the canoe.

A good anchor is almost always needed. If your streams require you to use it a lot, consider rigging up an efficient anchor system. Get a heavy cylinder-shaped anchor. A 10-pound, vinyl-covered, mushroom-shaped anchor will also do. Rig a pulley to the stern and pad a section of the outside of the stern, to protect the canoe and cut down on noise. Some thick vinyl tape will work as padding. This way you can let the anchor hang on the outside (against the padding) and raise and lower it by pulling the anchor rope through the pulley. Keep the extra rope close in front of you. This is a quick, quiet, and efficient anchoring system.

Different Seasons

ANYONE WHO WANTS TO BE a proficient year-round angler must understand the stream smallmouth's habits and locations during different seasons. Based on the climate and conditions of most of the smallmouth's range, this chapter covers the eight months from April through November, divided into five fishing periods. In the extreme southern edge of the range, this can be stretched into nine months, with the spring season starting in March and fall lingering into December. However, I haven't included a detailed midwinter fishing period, primarily because most of the smallmouth's range is locked in winter's frozen grip during this time. Trying to fish for bass that are in semihibernation during the cold, snow, and ice of January and February is extremely tough. Even in the warmest areas, like Arkansas, where the streams aren't iced over, the fishing is still pretty slow.

Please note that the five fishing periods are only generalized. The smallmouth range stretches over 750 miles from north to south, so these periods don't occur at exactly the same time everywhere. The different fishing periods are largely determined by *water* temperature, and the latitude of a stream isn't the only factor that determines its temperature. Some Mid-South mountain streams are at higher elevations, heavily shaded, and spring fed, and so they run cooler than waters farther north. Conversely, even some streams as far north as Ontario and Minnesota that are unshaded and have little spring water warm up quickly in the early summer. Use the calendar dates in this chapter as only approximate guidelines. Investigate the streams you plan to fish, and don't forget your thermometer.

The Five Fishing Periods

Period	Water Temperature Range	Calendar Dates (+ or − 2 weeks)
Spring/Prespawn	45° to 56°	April 1 to May 10
Spawn	57° to 65°	May 10 to June 5
Summer	65° plus	June 5 to August 10
Late summer/Early fall	70s or 80s to 55 or 60°	August 10 to September 20
Fall	55 or 60° to 44°	September 20 to November 20

SPRING/PRESPAWN PERIOD

- *Water Temperatures:* Beginning of period, 45 degrees; end, 56 degrees
- *Calendar Dates:* April 1 to May 10 (plus or minus two weeks)

This can be a fairly long period, lasting nearly two months in some areas. Angling success during this period is extremely weather dependent. The question of open or closed spring seasons will have to be debated elsewhere; here I'll stick with when smallmouth are biologically ready to be caught.

During the early part of the spring period, when the water is in the 40s, the stream smallie is still in a low-activity state – not completely inactive, but slow and sluggish. As the water warms into the low to mid 50s, the bass become increasingly active. Water temperatures below the mid-40s (either in the spring or fall) make for very slow fishing. A few people fish smallmouth down into the 30s, but I personally think it's too unproductive to be worth the effort. At 45 degrees fish can still be caught with regularity on artificials (if presented properly).

The dates these water temperatures occur vary from year to year. Throughout most of the range, April 1 is about the earliest that water temperatures will reach the upper 40s. In northern states, this early warm water occurs only when there is a dry warm spring, when river levels stay low, and there are lots of sunny days. In a more average spring, with higher water levels and less warm weather, water doesn't reach the upper 40s until mid-April. The date of the spring thaw and the amount of snow melt, spring rain, and sunny warm weather combine to determine the spring water temperatures. The basic rule of thumb is this: a warm and dry spring means an early season; a cold and wet spring means a late season.

Keep an eye on the streams you plan to fish. Watch water levels and clarity in addition to temperatures. In fact, inappropriate water levels and clarity can cancel out acceptable water temperatures. If a stream is in flood stage or absolutely turbid, fishing will probably be impossible even if the temperature is high. However, relatively low, clear water conditions often occur early in the spring before heavy spring rains. April often has a couple of weeks where many streams are in their banks, visibility is acceptable, and temperatures are at least in the upper 40s. Bass can be caught very well during this time. Then early May comes with heavy rains, and fishing is almost impossible for a while. So the smart angler keeps a close eye on stream conditions and heads to the water whenever those conditions say "fish"—not just when the calendar says a certain date.

Fish Locations

To find the fish, understand what their needs are. Coming out of winter slumber, the stream bass are first concerned with finding food and warmer water. As the water rises into the mid-50s, spawning becomes top priority. A fourth desire: to escape the strong currents so common in springtime. On the very smallest streams, the bass will be in or near many of the same wintering "holes" they have been in since fall. On larger waters, they'll move upstream; two favorite spots are below dams or at warmer creek mouths (if the current isn't too strong and the depth is sufficient). As spawning temperatures draw near, the fish will gravitate close to spawning areas. Earlier, they will probably be in slightly deeper water near their future spawning sites.

Angling Methods

Remember that the smallmouth is a very sluggish fish even at 50 degrees. (In comparison, a trout or pike at that temperature is almost a hyped-up maniac.) In the springtime, *slow and easy* is the name of the game. Keep your retrieves slow and pay close attention to soft strikes. The bass will strike but they won't chase your lure any distance. Dragging it in front of their noses, perhaps several times, pays off. It's important to find a concentration of fish, to make your patient efforts count. If water levels aren't too high (only a foot or two above summer levels) and the clarity and temperatures are acceptable, try a smaller creek. Look for deeper pools, especially ones that have lots of cover in and around them. If you hook a fish in one of these pools, fish that spot very thoroughly; there are almost certainly more close by.

In high water so common in spring (several feet above summer levels), bass can still be caught. The best location by far under these adverse conditions is below dams or falls, especially ones that have some calmer holding water. Again, thoroughly work the potential fish-holding areas, including dead-calm overflow areas and side pockets. The bass will try to avoid fighting the strong currents, either by moving to calmer side waters or going deep into rock protection on the bottom. The best time of day to fish during this early period is late afternoon and early evening.

As for lures, rarely does anything outperform the old lead head in the spring. Fished as slowly as possible, the lead-head jig is a consistent producer. Bright colors are generally best; white, orange, chartreuse, yellow, and silver tinsel are my favorites. Since much of the spring bass's diet is small fish, jigs that imitate minnows are often successful. Slow-moving spinners (mainly silver blades) will also produce sometimes.

Using the knowledge and methods mentioned here, I've had excellent fishing very early in the spring, catching good numbers of big smallmouth when most anglers seemed to consider it too early for fishing.

SPAWN PERIOD

- *Water Temperatures:* Beginning, 57 degrees; end, 65 degrees
- *Calendar Dates:* May 10 to June 5 (plus or minus two weeks)

The spawn period is short, seldom more than four weeks. It starts when significant numbers of fish move into or near their beds and ends when the males start to leave their beds and fry. If water temperatures fall significantly after spawning starts, the fish will temporarily delay their activities and the period will be prolonged.

Concern is sometimes raised about the effect of catching bass on their beds. This is a minor problem. By far the biggest danger to bass is catch-and-kill angling. So it's essential that people release their fish during all times of year. But anglers should be aware that *repeated* catching and releasing of spawning male bass, while it does not injure the fish, can interfere with reproductive success. Catching nest-guarding males several times can expose eggs or fry to preda-tors. (The males can be distinguished because they are generally smaller than the females.) But in lightly to moderately fished streams – which describes many waters – catching and quickly re-turning the bass to their beds has no impact on the numbers of fry raised.

Actual egg laying normally occurs after the water reaches 60 degrees, but the fish start to relate to their bedding areas when temperatures rise into the upper 50s. During this period, when the females are on or near their beds and before they actually lay their eggs, there's good fishing for big bass. Then comes a period after egg laying, lasting up to two weeks, when the smaller males can easily be caught on the beds.

Fish Locations

There still seems to be considerable confusion among anglers about where river and creek smallmouth actually spawn. Some people, including a few fishing writers, think that *all* stream bass migrate upstream or into little feeder creeks to spawn. Don't believe it. Stream bass spawn wherever they find acceptable bedding areas. Yes, in some rivers the fish are forced to travel long distances upstream, but bass in other waters move no more than a few yards, since good spawning sites are close to their summer homes.

Smallmouth need hard bottoms and slow currents to spawn. An eddy on the edge of a pool with a gravel bottom is good. So is a pebble bottom along the banks of a stream channel where the current isn't too strong and the depths are sufficient. A calm, protected area behind a log or boulder is best of all. Stream bass spawn in water as shallow as 10 or 12 inches and as deep as 4 feet, especially if the water is exceptionally clear.

Like lake bass, stream fish like to put their beds next to some type of cover, like logs, banks, or – most especially – big rocks. This cover is vital for successful reproduction. A large upstream boulder or log will act as a current buffer and protect eggs or fry from being swept away if the river rises and the current increases. Logs and boulders also afford the newly hatched fry a degree of protection from predators. Studies have shown that bigger (older) smallmouth normally choose the best, most protected spawning sites. Small (young) bass often choose poor, unprotected sites even when better ones are available. This should tell us three things. First, smallies are smart fish; they continue to learn as they get older. Second, the biggest bass will be in the best spawning sites. Third, it's essential to release these older fish because they are the most successful spawners.

Bass feed very little during actual spawning and are quite skittish. Don't believe the tales about all stream spawners being easy to catch. In clear, shallow water (common conditions on some streams) the fish will be ultra-wary.

Angling Methods

Because bass aren't really feeding during spawning, they must be teased into striking out of reflex or a desire to protect their spawning site. The smallmouth are also uneasy about being in relatively shallow, exposed conditions. You'll need plenty of caution and finesse. A good pair of polarized glasses is indispensable.

Cautiously approach a possible bedding area and carefully

look for the circular beds (probably light colored), especially right next to the stream banks. Smallmouth beds will be at least 10 or 12 inches in diameter (smaller circles are from other nest-building species like rock bass and sunfish). The bass themselves are hard to see unless you spook them and they go racing off. In very shallow, clear conditions, you'll need a well-planned and very sneaky approach. If you're on foot, don't be shy about hunkering down or crawling.

Since you have to tease the fish into striking, a bait that does this is what you're looking for. Surface lures are often the best. You can drop them – *very lightly* – above the bed and wiggle, jiggle, pop, or buzz them over the fish until they strike. Don't use anything large or noisy. Fly-rod poppers work great, as do the old reliable floating Rapala thin minnows. Just remember: don't pull the bait away from the bed too quickly. If the current sweeps the lure away too fast, get into a position where you can maintain the lure over the bed.

On larger waters, bank shooting (casting to the banks) from a boat can be very effective. Floaters should also keep noise to an absolute minimum and stay at least 35 feet from the fish. This period is a very good time to consistently catch lots of big bass on the surface.

SUMMER PERIOD

- *Water Temperatures:* 65 degrees or higher
- *Calendar Dates:* June 5 to August 10 (plus or minus two weeks)

Summer is the time when the streams are the stablest, the fish (almost all species) are most active, and the fishing is the most consistent. Starting some time in June, peaking in July (or late June on the southern edge of the range), and ending by late August, these golden days should be savored by veterans and beginners alike.

After spawning, the bass are hungry. Also, the water is warming into the upper 60s and 70s, keeping their metabolism high. Any high, discolored water of spring should have subsided and cleared, allowing you easy access to the feeding fish. And the food sources for the fish haven't yet increased to the point that they are stuffed most of the time (a very important factor).

All this adds up to the end of another myth – the myth that

The warm-water conditions of summer are good for wet wading and active fish.

the time to really get them is early in the season before summer arrives. This may be true on a few southern streams, which warm up so much and get so clear the bass actually become stressed during hot summer spells. But for most streams, summer angling success is very good. For instance, during a recent July I stood in Iowa's Turkey River, which registered a positively hot 86 degrees, and caught bass until my arms ached! The biggest problem I had that day was staying cool enough to keep fishing, since the weather was a very humid 95 degrees. Common sense should tell you to take it easy on these hot days so you don't suffer from overheating or dehydration.

Summer for the smallmouth starts as soon as the females have recovered from egg laying and the males have left their fry to fend for themselves. With rapidly rising temperatures, this may mean the water is already above 70 degrees; other years the water may still be in the mid-60s. Regardless, if the females have gone through their postspawn rest (lasting about a week) and the water is down and clear, that is the onset of good fishing. The lower temperatures of early summer keep the bass from launching into a feeding frenzy, but as the water rises into the mid-70s the fish feed heavily. Water that's too hot will seldom be a problem.

July is the premier summer month in most of the smallmouth's range. Barring heavy thunderstorms, which can mess up the fishing on individual watersheds, bass, walleye, catfish, pickerel, and panfish can all be caught very well during July. The first half of August is almost as good, but some time after mid-August the conditions change. Food sources become very high and temperatures fluctuate, forcing a shift in strategies.

Fish Locations

Summer bass spread out widely to spots that provide food and cover. They take their places based on a hierarchy; the biggest bass get the best places. The larger, deeper pools hold many of those big bass, but the undercuts, riffles, and midstream boulders also have plenty of fish.

The old truism that bass are deep during midday (deeper pools) and shallow in mornings and evenings (riffles) is true only half the time. At high noon on bright sunny days bass can some-

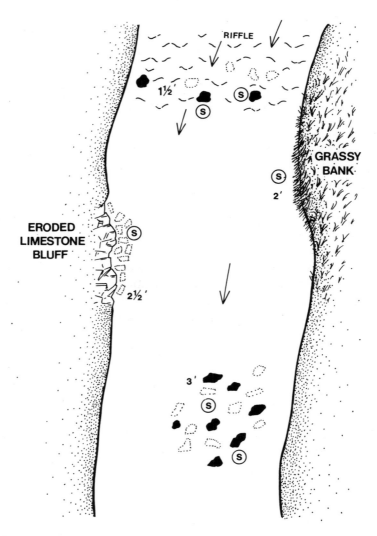

Smallmouth feeding areas. These common feeding spots are easy to identify and fish. Near eroded limestone outcroppings, pieces of stone have fallen into the stream.

times be found feeding actively in shallow water, especially in lower-visibility streams. So don't ignore the riffles or banks at mid-day, especially if the deeper water doesn't seem to produce well.

Angling Methods

With the high metabolism and active feeding habits of summer bass, you'll need a varied repertoire of angling tactics. Faster-paced fishing has its place in the summer. Faster retrieves, covering water quickly, are productive *at times.* Don't go overboard, though, and assume this method is always best; even in summer, I use slower methods most of the time. Bottom bumping and extra-slow and easy retrieves often prompt the most strikes. Be prepared to try various techniques.

Occasionally, the bass are noticeably active, and you can see them chasing baitfish. Times like this obviously call for faster-moving, minnow-imitating baits. Keep an eye out for minnows breaking the surface; this generally means a smallie is in pursuit. These days can turn into exciting times – hard, smashing strikes one after another. What a way to wear yourself out! But most of the time smallmouth are eating crawfish, a food source that increases tremendously in summer, and baits that represent them do better. The tried and true lead head (of many types), crawfish crankbaits, and even some spinners trigger the bass's crawfish-eating response. And don't deprive yourself of the fun of using topwaters in the evening. Even if the fish had no interest in surface baits during the day, summer evenings can still see lots of surface action.

LATE SUMMER AND EARLY FALL

- *Water Temperatures:* Beginning, 70s or 80s; end, 55 or 60 degrees
- *Calendar Dates:* August 10 to September 20 (plus or minus two weeks)

Think of this period as a transition time, with multiple aspects. The beginning of the period is similar to summer: the water is still warm, food is plentiful, and the fish are in many of their summer

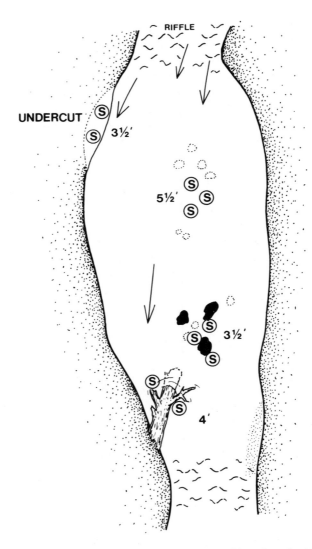

Smallmouth holding or resting areas. Partially submerged logs, large boulders, and the deep water of midpool are important fish-holding sites on most streams.

haunts, feeding heavily. As the season progresses (some time after September 1) water temperatures fall and the bass start changing their routines. Water levels are very low, causing extra-skittish fish. However, the main determining factor for the first part of the period is the plentiful food supply—or more accurately, the *overly* plentiful food supply. During late August and early September many waters have such an abundance of smallmouth food (especially crawfish) that angling becomes tough. Bass can certainly be caught, but a change in strategy is called for.

The beginning of this period can see water temperatures at their annual high—the mid-80s. Or in the North, they can already be falling. Either way, the populations of crawfish, minnows, and other bass food will still be very high.

The fishing at the end of this period will be *very dependent* on specific water temperatures in northern states. In fact, bass in more northern streams react dramatically to certain temperatures in the fall. Recent scientific studies have found that smallmouth migrate to wintering habitat as soon as the water hits a certain temperature. Only a few upper midwestern rivers and creeks have been carefully monitored, but definite patterns can be seen. In these northern waters, bass actually evacuate their summer residences when the water falls to 58 or 60 degrees, which can occur as early as the first week of September. Perhaps even more surprising, in some streams the bass actually migrate completely out of the stream. A Wisconsin Department of Natural Resources study found the smallmouth moving as much as 45 miles downstream into larger rivers.

These long-distance migrations probably take place only in upper midwestern, northern New England, and Canadian waters. In the rest of the range the fish don't seem to move nearly as far or as early. Smallmouth in streams at the latitude of northern Ohio generally don't move to wintering habitat until the water is 55 degrees. Also, in these waters wintering areas are probably just nearby deep pools or other places the fish can find calm water out of the current, although on shallow streams with only a few deeper pools, the bass will still travel a mile or so to one of these deeper areas. This should tell you it is vital to know when the late summer period has ended for these areas—and that it's impossible to use the calendar to determine the exact end of the period. Since the fish are so temperature-conscious at this time, only knowledge of water temperatures will enable you to know what's happening.

In the extreme southern edge of the range, fall patterns are the least pronounced. Streams in these areas cool down much more slowly and ultimately don't get as cold as waters farther north. The smallies in these waters haven't become genetically programmed to automatically seek out calm hibernating areas when the water hits a certain temperature, like their northern cousins have. Here the fish just move out of strong current areas and into calmer water pockets as they become more sluggish.

Fish Locations

During this time bass could be described as "fussy feeders." Where do you find these fussy fish? Wherever they were in the summer *if the water is still deep enough.* During normal years the water levels have probably dropped to the point where some riffles, and even some pools, no longer hold fish. No decent-sized bass, that is; little 6-inchers are probably still scattered everywhere. That means the fish are a little concentrated – but unfortunately, so is much of their food, making easy pickings for the fish.

Angling Methods

To sum up, the well-fed fish aren't really hungry. What to do? Give them something that stands out from the crowd! This means baits with lots of size, visibility, and "noise," or ones presented in such a slow and tantalizing way they can't refuse. Some bottom-bumping crankbaits seem to generate the kind of noise or vibration that make the bass take notice. It's important to use crankbaits that run with the tail of the plug almost straight up to reduce hangups. Plugs with some crawfish color are best – orange, rust, and browns.

Another favorite bait for this period are the ones I call "crawfish plus" – crawfish-imitating jigs that are bigger and more tantalizing than the real thing. "Soft" jigs of the pork and plastic variety are good. Large, double-tailed plastic-bodied jigs in the 3½-inch size are deadly. Mounted on the lightest jig head that conditions will allow (either 1/16 or 1/8 ounce), this "crawfish plus" can be slowly swum and hopped right by a bass's nose. A lead head with a modified pork frog or pork crawdad also accomplishes this. Refer to the chapter on spinning lures for more detail on jigs with an extra-soft or natural feel to them. Whatever type jig you use, work it slowly on the bottom. Weed-guard–equipped jigs will sometimes be needed to cut down snagging.

FALL PERIOD

- *Water Temperatures:* Beginning, 55 to 60 degrees; end, 44 degrees
- *Calendar Dates:* September 20 to November 20 (plus or minus two weeks)

This is a unique period, often misunderstood by anglers and some writers. An old cliché says that all black bass are in a feeding frenzy in the fall. What actually happens is this: as temperatures drop the bass's metabolism and feeding rates slow. At the same time, food sources become scarce and the bass become more concentrated as they move into their winter residences. This means good fishing can be had, but only if you use techniques appropriate for these conditions.

Let's break this down a little further and look at what's happening in specific parts of the fish's range in the fall. We'll start by dividing the range into two zones, the northern third and the southern two-thirds. The most northern (or coldest) streams are inhabited by smallmouth that move downstream (sometimes many miles) when the water reaches a certain temperature. Depending on the individual waterway, that trigger temperature can be as high as 60 degrees. They move to get into a "hibernaculum," a place where they can stay until spring, burning as few calories as possible. After arriving at these winter residences, the bass still feed a little, but as the temperature falls so does the fish's activity until they become almost dormant. A would-be angler faces a major problem on streams of this type. The bass may be in only a handful of deep pools or may have moved completely out of a small stream. Unless you are already familiar with the wintering areas I'd recommend you avoid fall angling on these streams.

Late fall fishing, while productive, can require plenty of warm clothes. Note the fingerless gloves—they keep your hands warm and give you the dexterity you need for casting. Lyn Verthein.

In the other two-thirds of the continental range finding fall bass isn't nearly as difficult. The fish generally don't migrate long distances, but just shift to the best resting areas they can find nearby, which may only be 10 yards downstream. (In very shallow stretches, less than 3 feet deep, the fish may still move several hundred yards downstream.) Bass in these streams are more concentrated than they are in summer and can be caught if their slow metabolism is taken into account.

In the northern edge of the range the fall period starts around 59 degrees. For most other areas, it's in the mid-50s. I put the end of the period at 44 degrees. Below this the fish are so sluggish, feed so infrequently, and fight so weakly that fishing loses its appeal for most people. One important thing to remember about small-stream temperatures is their daily fluctuation. In the fall, water temperatures can drop to 40 degrees at night but climb to the upper 40s by midafternoon. So even if early-morning temperatures are too cold for good fishing, the water may warm up enough in the afternoon to energize the bass. Larger waters don't fluctuate this much but still have some up and down movement of daily temperatures. In any size river, midafternoon is the best time for fall fishing.

Fish Locations

Actually finding specific holding areas that contain fall bass can be perplexing. In the coldest regions, smallmouth can move long distances, and even in other areas they occupy only a portion of their normal summer habitat. Finding the exact location of the fish is the key to success. Head to the deepest pools in the stretch of river that you *already* know has some good pools, with deep and slow current. On a small creek these pools may only be 4 feet deep; in a larger river they will probably be over 6 feet. If there is any cover, like downed trees or boulders, in a deep pool, so much the better. The holding water doesn't have to be large; a few square yards can hold more than a dozen bass. In some streams there may be over a dozen bass-holding areas per mile; shallower waters may have only one per mile. The smallmouth in very shallow rivers are actually quite vulnerable in the fall because they are so concentrated.

Angling Methods

Fall smallmouth are slow and sluggish. They want their meals in small bites and presented slowly in front of their noses. Find a likely-looking pool and work it *slowly*. Try a small jig (dark-colored) and hop it along the bottom extra slow. A minnow-tipped jig is often very good. Use line that's as light and limp as possible. Pay very, very close attention to your line as the jig settles to the bottom. Fall fish can inhale a jig with amazing lightness. If you even suspect a strike, set the hook!

When the water is above 50 degrees, slow-moving spinners sometimes produce, but in very cold water the jig nearly always excels. (Fly fishers should use weighted nymphs or other deep-working flies.) If you work a pool thoroughly and get no strikes, don't hang around; move on quickly to a different one. If you do strike paydirt, work the water extra thoroughly, because that bass most certainly isn't alone.

Some extremely large smallmouth can be caught from their fall holes. The fish are at their maximum annual size and are highly concentrated. Whatever you do, *don't* destroy the fishing quality of an entire section of stream by killing off its big bass in the fall. Cropping off the big bass in one pool can mean several miles of stream the following year won't have many large fish. By all means get out and enjoy some late-season fishing, but release them so we can all have good fishing the next year.

7

Fishing in Difficult Water Conditions

ALL RIVER ANGLERS HAVE TO STRUGGLE with the frustrations of tough fishing conditions, and not all unfavorable conditions can be overcome easily. So, let's be bold and start with the toughest situations first, then work our way down to the less troublesome ones.

LOW-VISIBILITY WATER

Low-visibility water can have several causes; the three main ones are turbid (muddy) conditions, bog-stained waters, and heavy algae growth.

Muddy Water

Muddy water means water that has heavy amounts of suspended soil caused by erosion. In many streams in the Farm Belt, this is a common problem. It is also the hardest water condition to success-fully deal with. Water that is absolutely turbid, with zero visibility, means almost zero angling success. Even bottom fishing with live bait catches very few fish when the streams are too turbid. When a specific waterway is extremely muddy, it's best to go elsewhere. (A little later, we'll look at some ways to find out beforehand when rivers are muddy or high.)

The good news about muddy conditions is that they don't last forever. Many streams remain very turbid for only a day or two after a heavy rain before the water starts to clear. Bass and other species can be caught at this time because the water is no longer extremely muddy, only murky. Murky water visibility is still low (less than a foot), but the fish have probably adjusted to it and are feeding a little. Some smallmouth may have even moved back to normal feeding areas like the bottom of riffles; others may still be "sitting" in the bottom of pools. Try both areas.

All your angling under these murky water conditions should be *slow*. (Murky water is somewhat roiled by runoff, but is clearer than muddy water.) You don't necessarily need slow retrieves, but slowly and thoroughly work a particular area by making multiple casts to each spot. Bigger, higher-visibility, noisy baits are called for. Flashy in-line spinners and spinner baits are good. Some streams in the East and in the Midwest run murky through much of the spring and early summer. The fish in these waters have had to adapt to low-visibility conditions as an almost permanent aspect of

Lowering your silhouette by crouching during your approach allows you to get closer to the fish without spooking them. Lyn Verthein.

their life. Higher-visibility, noisy lures produce well, but it's surprising how often quiet, drab, "normal" baits also produce in these "dirty" streams. Maybe the fish's eyesight gets keener under these conditions.

Heavily Stained Water

A permanent type of low-visibility water is the waterways stained from bog drainage. Because of the natural, stained runoff from adjacent bogs and lowlands, these streams *never* become very clear. Such drainages are located in various areas in the United States and Canada but are most common in the northern regions. The most heavily stained ones appear to have a visibility of only a few inches, even in their clearest periods. Other less stained waters clear up substantially during late summer dry spells. Regardless, all bog-stained waters are fishable. The fish have adapted to the poor-visibility conditions and go about their regular routines, even though you and I may think little activity is possible.

The biggest problem with this type of stream is not the fish finding your bait, but you finding the fish. Bog waters are quite infertile. Their chemistry keeps them low in food, so they have lower numbers of bass. However, many dark-watered streams can still provide fine angling. Using techniques tailored to these conditions, you should be able to catch and release enough smallmouth, pickerel, pike, and walleye to have a very enjoyable outing.

Because of the relatively low populations of fish in these dark waters, your strategy should be to cover as much water as possible. Floating or wading, work likely areas quickly. Even though the water visibility seems poor, the fish seem to strike fairly quickly. (They're probably extra hungry in these low-food, infertile waters.) A few casts to a target area will probably be enough to entice any fish interested. Keep moving until you hit fish. If you catch one from a spot, work that area more thoroughly; two or three fish from a single pool is realistic. Then move on, looking for another mini-concentration of fish.

If the river you are fishing is large enough, float it; wading in dark-watered streams can be difficult. Seeing what is below the surface is almost impossible, so it's easy to trip on subsurface rocks.

It's especially hard in streams that are filled with dark-colored, smooth, igneous rock. If you do wade, move carefully in the water and do your faster traveling on the banks.

What types of lures produce under these heavily stained conditions? The most unusual types of baits for these waters, black-bladed spinners, are often effective. Other dark baits like black jigs also produce. But don't rely solely on them. I do very well on more conventional spinners, primarily ones with large gold (brass) blades. Gold-bladed spinner-flies with large flies are very good. Adding a ripple rind trailer is even btter. Also try shallow-running crankbaits with lots of vibration and flash.

Heavy Algae Growth

As the summer progresses, some waterways experience a heavy growth of algae, especially brown algae, usually caused by agricultural nutrients. This gives the water a somewhat muddy or murky appearance even when it hasn't rained in weeks. Fortunately, the algae itself seems to have little detrimental effect on the fish or the fishing. So don't be turned off by brownish-looking midsummer waterways. The smallmouth's vision is restricted a little, but otherwise they feed and react like fish in clear water. Fish a little slower (a few more casts to a likely spot) and give them bigger, more visible baits.

HIGH WATER AND STRONG CURRENTS

"High water" means significantly above normal summer levels for a particular waterway. Small creeks can generally be regarded as high when they are 12 to 18 inches above summer levels; for larger rivers, it might be 2 or 3 feet. It's mainly a question of how much increased water it takes before the fish alter their routines and change their positions, so that anglers must adopt new techniques. Invariably, current speeds are increased with higher water flows, further complicating angling.

Let's look at the problem of high water and strong currents

when they occur in summer. (The high water of spring is different: the water temperatures are much colder, the fish are preparing to spawn, and the high-water conditions last longer.) When summer rivers first start to rise, bass fishing is poor even if the water hasn't muddied up. When the water has risen and stabilized, fishing will pick up, especially if the river has also cleared up somewhat from its murkiness. Slowly falling levels are also okay, but rapidly falling water is poor.

Changes in the Bass's Behavior

It's thought by many that when stream smallmouth are faced with rapidly rising water and increased currents, they "hole up" behind deep-water obstructions and don't feed. But how do they adjust to a *period* of higher flows and currents? In many streams, they move near the banks and into the mouths of small tributaries. This gets them out of the strong currents of midchannel and puts them near food.

Many minnow species move into flooded bank vegetation or flooded tributary mouths at this time. The bass that follow them can be caught by various minnow imitations, especially bright spinners. Newly created quiet eddies on the edges of pools are also worth trying. These temporary holding spots can be over areas that normally are very shallow or otherwise fishless. Pike or pickerel are also in these high-water areas and will occasionally be taken along with bass. Lures and lines can be a little heavier under these conditions. In fact, with the reduced visibility and faster currents, larger and heavier baits generally work better.

It's easy to figure out the pattern that smallmouth establish in the sections of waterways influenced by power dam discharges. The fishing downstream of a hydroelectric power dam is almost always the best when the levels are in their lower stages. When the water starts to rise, fishing can still be good for a while. But when the flow rates approach their peak, fish shut off. After the heavy flows subside, the bass and other species once again start striking. So avoid the maximum water levels below power dams. Give the power company a call to find out when the plant releases water (it's generally at the same times every day); then compute when that water will reach your fishing area.

Predicting High-Water Conditions

To successfully fish any river it's important to know what the river is doing before you get to it. There are several ways to find out. The best way, of course, is to call someone who has accurate, updated information on water levels and clarity. However, information of this sort isn't always easy to come by on most smaller warm-water streams. A knowledgeable person who lives near the stream, or state fisheries personnel or enforcement officers (game wardens) are good sources. Your state may have a number to call that will give water levels on rivers large enough to float. You can also find out the rainfall amounts in the area from local radio stations and newspapers, and use this to predict the river's condition. You get the idea: do a little advance work and save yourself lots of grief. You could also have a few alternative waters on standby in case your favorite one is unfishable.

VERY LOW OR CLEAR WATER

Very low or very clear water can be either a stimulating challenge or an absolute pain to fish. If you're the sort who hates having to change tactics or routine, dealing with a very low or clear stream will be pure frustration. If you get enjoyment out of doing well under less than optimum conditions, this is for you. Personally, I think this attitude of enjoying occasional extra challenges should be part of all sport angling. Actually, these conditions can be dealt with more easily than high or muddy water.

Very Clear Water

I call a stream clear when you can stand on a low bank and easily see the bottom in 4 feet of water, or if you can see the bottom directly beneath you while floating in 5 feet of water. Some waterways never get that clear, others do only occasionally in the fall, and a few run that clear nearly all the time. When the water clarity is that high, our pal the smallmouth becomes one wary fish. Smallies seem to be able to sense an angler a hundred yards away (well, maybe not *that* far) and greet all your presentations with careful scrutiny. Under these circumstances you should treat the stream smallmouth like you would heavily fished stream trout. I've fished a number of streams where the elusive brown trout lived with the smallmouth, and the bass were at least as difficult to catch as the trout.

Extra-Careful Approaches

To get these tricky characters, apply plenty of common stream sense, like extra-careful approaches. Sneaking is mandatory when the fish can spot you so easily. Get as low as possible! Use trees, bushes, tall grass, and boulders to cover your on-foot approach to a casting position. Stay farther away from your target than you would otherwise, no matter whether you're on foot or in a craft. Obviously, this calls for longer casts. Take your time getting into position and stay longer at one place. Let the fish calm down in case they did detect you. Standing, kneeling, or sitting quietly for fifteen minutes in one place can pay off in strikes you never would have gotten if you had left after five minutes.

Delicate Presentations

Along with those careful approaches, use delicate presentations—no loud *kersplashes* when your lure hits the water. If possible, cast quite a ways past your target, to keep the splash away. Use light lines or light leaders and small lures. *Small lures are very important.* Normal or larger-sized bass baits are often totally rejected in extra-clear water. Tiny plugs of various sorts only an inch or so long can produce strikes when larger stuff is ignored. The same with lead heads and spinner-fly combos. Go down to the little sizes and the more natural colors with low flash. Often the best colors for plastic-tailed jigs are smoke or motor oil. These hard-to-see colors may not be worth a hoot in less clear water, but in crystal-clear conditions they may be the only thing that fools the bass. This is also one of the few times 2-pound test line comes in handy, but stay with 4-pound if snags are a problem or if the fish run large.

One of the most effective things you can do on clear-water streams is fish during low-visibility periods. It's not always possible, but fishing on dark cloudy days or in early mornings or late evenings really helps. In the last hour of daylight the ultrawary daytime bass often throws caution to the wind and strikes with almost reckless abandon.

Very Low Water

Very low flow conditions sometimes, but not always, go with extra-clear conditions. Even if the stream doesn't become extra clear, the fish will react to the low flow rates. All species are forced to concentrate and often become stressed and skittish when their living space shrinks around them. You can probably tell if a stream is extra low if all the bank vegetation is high above the water line. Low flows usually develop during long dry spells, but can also be caused by upstream dams sharply restricting their discharges.

At the start of a low water period, the predator fish may be very tough to catch. Besides being skittish in the newly restricted habitat, they have abundant food for a while because minnows and

Vertical jigging is a good technique around large logs that are in fairly deep, low-visibility water.

crawfish have been forced to concentrate in the remaining water, too. If the low flows continue, the fish adjust to it somewhat and food becomes scarcer (it's eaten faster than it's produced). Now the fish can be caught if you adjust to the conditions.

I recently fished a stream that had been affected by a long-term drought. For weeks this intermediate-sized stream had been reduced to a small creek with only a few pools over 2 feet deep. In the last thirty minutes of daylight, my partner and I caught and released twenty-eight smallies, walleye, and big rock bass from one small pool. The fish were very concentrated and hungry, but also very cautious. It took near-darkness before we could entice them into striking.

Be very careful in your fishing. Use cautious approaches and presentations. Sometimes hooking and then fighting a fish will spook the other ones in the area. If possible, lead the hooked fish downstream, away from the main concentration of fish.

The most difficult aspect of low-water fishing may be actually finding the fish. You may have to travel several hundred yards to find a single place that holds fish. Previous knowledge of the waterways pays off now. Think of where the deepest pools, glides, and undercuts are and head for them. If the stream is new to you, daytime scouting lets you see if there is sufficient water in a particular spot to warrant fishing. Then, if you can, come back to these areas in the morning or evening, just as you would on an extra-clear stream. If you do try during midday, fish deep with small baits.

WEEDY CONDITIONS

Unfortunately, a few smallmouth streams experience a significant amount of summer weed growth. But fortunately, even the waterways with the heaviest aquatic vegetation are almost never as weedy as many lakes. So you won't have to use one of those abominable ultraheavy-action rods so common to lake anglers. Most of the vegetation encountered in northern smallmouth waters is narrow, grassy plants commonly known as eel grass, because of their long, narrow shape. Eel grass grows in clumps several feet long and trails downstream, undulating from side to side in the current. When fishing near weeds, you will have to take the movement of the vegetation into account when casting and retrieving around it.

Weed growth in the northern two-thirds of the smallmouth range isn't normally significant before July 1. In more southerly streams, weed growth can occur a few weeks earlier. Mid-South streams also have a different type of aquatic vegetation, a stiff-stemmed plant that grows in dense strips in a foot or so of water along the banks. This vegetation is impossible to miss since it's quite dense and protrudes out of the water several inches, with small purple flowers during the summer. However, this shallow-water vegetation doesn't have much influence on the fishing, except occasionally during the summer when bass feed for minnows along the edges of these weed strips.

Overall, the river smallmouth's relationship to weed growth in its environment (north or south) isn't particularly close. Bass don't seem to seek out weeds, but simply adjust to them if they occur. On the other hand, "river rockets" (stream pike, pickerel, and muskie) definitely gravitate toward weed growth. If thick clumps or patches of eel grass do grow up in an area where a smallmouth resides, it will often use them as cover. It won't go deep into the weeds like a pike may, but will lie downstream where the grass "tails" out. This should tell you that being able to see exactly where the weeds are and where they end is important. I like to fish weeds under bright conditions with polarized glasses so I can see them clearly. Look for pockets and channels in the weeds, keeping in mind the tendency of the fish to lie in the tail pockets.

Weed-Fishing Baits and Techniques

Unless you use topwaters, weedless (or at least semiweedless) baits are required for eel grass fishing. Don't expect to use your regular crankbaits or in-line spinners. The Mepps Combo (a weedless plastic tail on a regular spinner) is pretty good. So are small ⅛-ounce safety-pin spinners if you fish them carefully. Don't chuck them smack into the middle of weed clumps. Keep them near the surface till you bring the lure into a pocket, where you should let it flutter down 18 inches or so. Watch carefully for the strike as the lure falls. Even lightweight, long-tailed plastic-bodied jigs can sometimes be

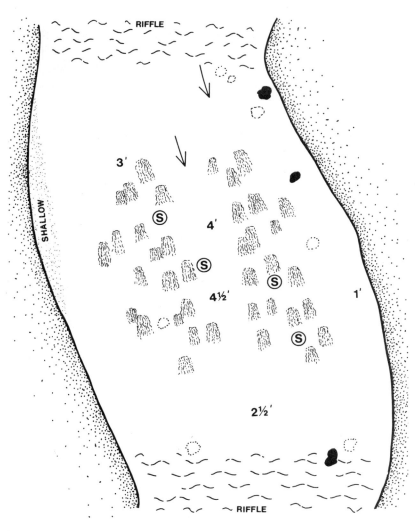

Stringy aquatic vegetation growing in clumps is common in some streams. Smallmouth tend to position themselves at the downstream end of these clumps. Accurate casts (with the aid of polarized glasses) can target these holding pockets.

used in this same way, provided they're equipped with a soft weed guard. A 7-foot rod rated about light-medium action with 8-pound test line will really shine for this type of work. If the current isn't too stiff, a nearly unweighted pork eel or short, extra-soft plastic worm on a weedless hook can be drifted and retrieved past the clumps and let flutter into pockets.

A fly rod in the right hands will pay off handsomely around the weeds. If you can get close enough to just lay your fly down and pick it back up without a long retrieve, you can cover lots of spots without hanging up in the weeds. Working various streamer patterns near the surface or poppers in these clearings in the "forest" is effective.

One final comment on river weed fishing: in the northern half of the range, some time in September (occasionally as early as late August) the vegetation starts to die and break free, and increasing amounts of it start to float downriver. In some places the weeds literally become large floating rafts of debris. Fishing with almost anything at the peak of the breakup is almost impossible; head to less weedy streams during this couple of weeks.

8

Spinning Tackle and Equipment

NOT ENOUGH GOOD INFORMATION is available on appropriate *stream* tackle. This chapter aims to fill that gap by giving you solid recommendations based solely on stream fishing needs. And the tackle suggested isn't expensive; buying a complete outfit need entail only modest outlays of cash.

What tackle do you need for streams? I'll break it down into specific areas, but one overall theme is the need to go light. Stream fishing requires lighter rods and lines than most anglers use for other types of fishing. For one thing, light rods, lines, and lures are the most practical for stream fishing. Some of the best spinning lures for streams are quite lightweight, $1/16$ ounce or even less. Light lines and light-action rods are needed to cast these baits any distance or with any degree of accuracy. And the action on many of these small lures is good only with light lines, 6 pounds or less. Second, by using a light rod you get a much better fight out of every fish hooked. Even a 10-inch smallmouth is great fun to catch on very light tackle. Using the more common medium-action rod and 8- or 10-pound line really limits the excitement.

Incidentally, this chapter is entitled "spinning" tackle very deliberately. Bait-casting outfits, no matter how light you try to make them, are still not adequate for *general* stream use. Under some specialized situations, like a river filled with wood snags and lots of large fish, geared-down bait-casting rigs may be fine, but these are the exception rather than the rule. I will primarily discuss open-

The "Compleat Angler," with long spinning rod, hip boots, hat, and well-stocked vest.

faced spinning reels and rods, since they work better than closed-face (spin-cast) tackle and are more popular for light river fishing.

SPINNING RODS

The most important part of your equipment is that stick you wave in the air all day. With all the casting and hook setting you do during a day on the stream, a good rod is critical. The most efficient and versatile stream bass rod is a 7-foot, light-action graphite model. These longer rods give you better line and lure control and better hook-setting ability. A 6½-footer, while not quite as good, will still perform adequately. The light action is stiff enough for good hook setting, but light enough to really throw those little baits and let the fish give you a great fight. In discussing rod action, use the standard grades manufacturers give their factory-made models. Look for light-action-rated rods that have most of their flex in their upper half (often described as having a "fast" tip) and are fairly stiff in the lower half. Avoid "spaghetti" rods—ones with flex from tip to butt; they're worthless.

These recommendations are based on many years of fishing, using various rods. I know many "experts" today emphasize muscle rods. They use pool cues with guides that can handle heavy baits and lines, "cross their eyes" when they set the hook, and bring the fish to hand in seconds. Unfortunately, this infatuation with heavy-duty tackle has influenced areas of angling, like stream fishing, where it serves no good purpose. Worst of all, the no-nonsense types seem to take the view that fighting a fish is a waste of time, because during this time they aren't casting to another fish. Well, I think fighting the fish is the best and most exciting part of angling. I'm not going to deprive myself of the enjoyment of winning (or sometimes losing) a good battle with every fish I hook. Long, light rods are very practical for stream angling. And they also make fishing far more enjoyable.

If you fish a lot and on a variety of stream types, you may want to consider adding two more rods to your collection. An ultra light model, at least 6½ feet long, is really nice on the little open creeks or even large open rivers that don't have a lot of big fish. Under these circumstances you won't be throwing any big baits or wrestling many hogs out of heavy cover. A whippy stick of this type is also a perfect stream trout and panfish rod.

The other rod to consider would be a little heavier one – a light-medium action, also in the longer lengths. With it you can use bigger and heavier baits and fish waters with lots of cover, especially weeds. Rivers with high numbers of pike or other large fish would also warrant this kind of rod.

Fishing *specifically* for larger river pike, muskie, or catfish is another ballgame altogether. (The chapter on bonus catches discusses tackle appropriate for that type of angling.) Also, a few creek anglers like to use a short 5- or 5½-foot rod on very brushy small streams. Even under these conditions, I don't think the short rods are desirable. But if you really worry about breaking a long rod on a stream of this kind, give the short rod a try.

Be aware that your local tackle shop may not carry a 7-footer, but good shops will order one for you. Many manufacturers make a wide variety of rod types and lengths. Don't be intimidated by the short-rod bias of the retail shops; ask them to order a decent long rod, order one yourself through the mail, or make your own. Nowadays, custom rod building is easy and increasingly popular. Find a shop that carries appropriate rod blanks, other rod materials, and good advice.

Never use a rod with any nicks in the guides. Nowadays with ceramic guides this isn't a big problem, but it still pays to check your guides periodically. Small-diameter lines (6-pound test or less) will be cut quickly by any nicks or grooves on the guides or the line guide on the reel. Replace the nicked part at once.

FISHING LINE

Of course, another basic element of any stream-fishing outfit is the line. My favorite all-purpose line strength is 6-pound test. It's light enough to handle most small lures well but still has enough muscle to take a hard day's fishing. Four-pound test would be my second favorite. I know some people who swear by 8-pound test. But I think you sacrifice too much by making 8-pound your all-purpose line. Too many lightweight lures don't cast very well on 8-pound, and the actions of many baits are impaired using this heavier, stiffer line. This line certainly has its place – say, when you're using mostly larger lures and focusing on bigger bass or other larger fish, or fishing in lots of weeds or heavy wood cover – but not for general-purpose use.

Going down in strength, 4-pound line is almost a necessity for tiny baits or very clear water. In extreme cases even 2-pound test can come in handy. A note of caution: if you have never or only rarely used anything lighter than 8-pound test, stick with 6-pound for a couple of months. Very light lines require some getting used to. If you can fish day after day with 6-pound without many breakoffs, then you are probably ready to try 4-pound line. Remember to set your drag carefully and check that last few feet of line regularly.

The experienced, versatile person carries three spools – 4-, 6-, and 8-pound test. Here's an example of how you might use the different types. Moving up the stream, you come upon an open pool where the bass (walleye, crappie, sunfish, or whatever) are interested only in very small jigs. Pop your 4-pound spool in and you are ready to go. As you progress along the stream to more typical situations, you can go back to the more popular 6-pound line. Later in the day, you drive over to a weed-filled river, and now the 8-pound is the right stuff. Different situations call for different lines.

Recently, low-stretch, cofilament lines have gained popularity. They're okay, but a more important line feature is limpness. I think even high-stretch lines that are extra limp will give your baits more action and allow you to feel more strikes.

No matter what type of light line you use, check it continually while fishing. Even small abrasions on a small-diameter line will cause a breakoff. I know an old-timer who uses 14-pound test and ties on a lure in May and seems to fish till September without retying. (Incidentally, he doesn't do very well most of the time.) Anyone who would do that with 6-pound would have nothing but aggravation. Check that last few feet of line carefully. It takes only a few seconds to clip off a foot and retie your bait. Even the puny 4-pound test will hold up to a day's fishing if you're diligent about checking it.

Over a season of heavy use you should replace the line on each reel spool at least three times. Put backing on the spools so you need only 50 yards of good line to fill the spool. This will be plenty for casting, and it's a lot quicker and cheaper to replace 50 rather than 150 yards.

SPINNING REELS

The best type of open-faced spinning reel for stream use is a quality, smaller-sized model with a large-diameter spool and at least a 5:1 retrieve ratio. I've seen too many cheap models literally fall apart in a few weeks of hard use. Remember, a stream angler using artificials will make a tremendous number of casts in a day's fishing. Your reel has to stand up to this heavy use.

I like smaller-sized models because they aren't cumbersome and tiring to use all day. But be sure to get a large-diameter spool; it allows much easier and longer casting. Several manufacturers now market smaller-sized models with oversized spools. A 5:1 gear ratio will enable you to pick up loose line quickly and bring your bait back fast when you need to.

A good drag on your reel is also a significant consideration. With 8-pound test your reel drag often doesn't matter, but with 4-pound it certainly does. Make sure the drag is always smooth and never freezes up. Or you can avoid breaking your line by "back reeling." With this method, you render your drag inoperative by tightening it completely and never using the antireverse. Experience will teach you when to give line by reeling backward. I use this method for nearly all types of fishing (including light saltwater spinning); I can apply exactly the amount of pressure I want to the fish. Try back reeling only if you are experienced in using light lines and fighting lots of bass or other strong fish.

Another important aspect of a good reel is the availability of parts and service, especially spare parts. Get extra spools and bail springs when you buy a reel so they are there when you need them. And make sure other parts can be ordered easily and quickly. No matter how well made, a reel will occasionally need replacement parts.

If you want to use spin-cast rods and reels, follow the basic guidelines for open-faced tackle. Look for long, light rods and well-made reels with a very good drag.

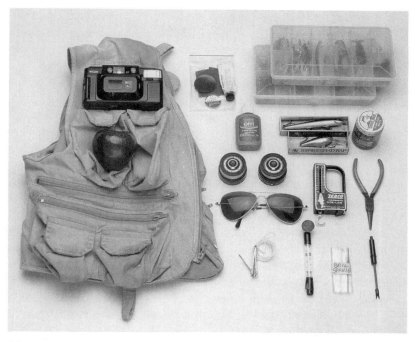

Many things should go into a well-stocked vest: lure boxes, pork baits, pliers, scale, hook hone, extra bail springs, thermometer, clippers, polarized glasses, extra reel spools, insect repellent, boot repair kit, and camera. The apple for lunch is optional. Sheldon Bolstad.

OTHER NECESSITIES

Some people hit the streams in their sneakers with only a rod and a couple of lures in their pocket. But I don't believe being this poorly equipped is adequate. To really fish streams, you need a few things besides a rod, reel, and lure: boots or waders, a vest, and several vest items. Compared to the cost of the lake angler's boat, motors, and electronics, a stream fisher's equipment expenses are negligible.

Boots or Waders

A good pair of hip boots is almost as important as your rod. Without it you are shackled to the bank or forced to get wet, cold, or muddy. Hip boots are much better for general use than chest-high waders because they are easier to walk in. A stream angler does a lot of dry-land walking, and comfortable footwear is essential. Many streams are also fairly shallow, and careful wading in hip boots will enable you to cover most of the water.

Chest waders, while not as easy to walk in and hot in the summer, certainly have their place. They are essential for deep-water areas and they are often useful on rivers where thick, brushy banks force you to stand in the deeper water of midstream. Fly rodders are more prone to needing chest waders, since they need to get farther away from the banks to cast.

If you can start out by buying a pair of both hip boots and chest waders, by all means do so; just make sure they are the uninsulated type. If you can afford only one type of wading boot, go with the hip boots (unless you plan to confine yourself to deeper waters). Good-quality boots will run about $50 and chest waders at least $15 more. The cheaper imported brands won't hold up to even moderate use. Better brands should last at least six or seven years, probably eight to ten with moderate use.

For those few streams that have beds with high amounts of extremely smooth and slippery rocks, felt-soled boots or waders give better grip than regular rubber-soled footwear. But they wear out more quickly and will have to be replaced after two or three dozen trips. One good way to get long life out of your felt-soled boots is to replace the felt yourself. Good low-cost felt remnants can be obtained from a carpet store. Simply cut felt pieces that match the boot soles and use industrial-strength glue to secure them to the boot.

Nowadays, nylon boots and waders are becoming more popular than ones made solely of rubber. Nylon footwear is lighter weight and cooler than rubber, but even the best quality nylon still isn't quite as tough or tear-resistant as rubber. So if you fish around a lot of potential boot snags (like barbed-wire fences and sharp thorns) rubber boots are still your best bet. If you plan on using chest-high waders quite a bit, quality nylon waders will pay off with their added comfort and coolness.

Let's talk a little about "wet wading." In northern climes, wading without boots or chest highs is comfortable only for several weeks in midsummer (a few weeks more in southern regions), so it isn't a year-round substitute for boots. But when the water is in at least the 70s and the air in the 80s, wading wet can be very nice. Shorts and sandals are okay when there is no brush or other scratchy vegetation to walk through. On most waterways, lightweight, fast-drying long pants (forget the heavy denim jeans) and jogging shoes are more practical. If you wade in jogging shoes, make sure they allow water to drain out easily when you get out of the river.

Vests

Another necessity is an all-purpose fishing vest. If you plan to carry more than the lure tied on your line and a couple of sinkers in your pocket, you need a vest. Even while float fishing, a vest is superior to a tackle box, especially if you get out of your craft to fish on foot. Get one with several large outside pockets, two inside ones, a very large back pocket, and a number of smaller ones. Make sure all pockets can be shut securely so items won't be lost. You don't have to get an $80 vest; one costing half that is acceptable as long as it has enough pocket space.

In a vest with plenty of pockets, one or two small pockets can be used as a place to dry lures. An empty pocket is a good place to put wet jigs, flies, and spinner-flies so they can dry before putting them back into their boxes. The sheepskin patch on vests is a *bad* place to dry or carry lures because they will fall off and be lost. If treble-hooked spinner-flies catch in the vest material, just line the carrying pocket with a piece of soft vinyl to eliminate the problem.

Some of the items you'll need in your vest are: two to four plastic lure boxes, a small needle-nosed pliers, hook hone, line clippers, and extra reel spools. A few more necessities are a good pocket tape and scale, extra bail springs, thermometer, polarized sunglasses, insect repellent, and a small boot repair kit. Add a few bandaids and a small flashlight (if you plan to fish late in the evening). Needless to say, all these items should be as light and compact as possible (no bulky aerosol can of repellent). Even with all these items, a good vest will still have room for some near-essentials like a small camera, a lunch, compact binoculars, or mushroom identification book.

Aside from some specific lures (covered in the next chapter), you're now a well-equipped moving-water angler. In fact, with the basic gear described here you will be equipped to comfortably fish almost any of the thousands of wadable smallmouth or trout streams on the continent.

9

Spinning Lures

SOME PEOPLE QUICKLY TURN to this part in fishing books, passing over the "inconsequential" stuff like good angling techniques. Resist this "get rich quick" attitude; a few hot lures will not substitute for learning solid fishing skills. While the proper type of enticement on the end of the line is important, knowing why, where, when, and how to use them is of much greater value. If you develop good "stream sense" you can make a fair showing with even lousy baits. With the best lures *and* good techniques, you'll clean up!

Let me tell you about the little lure experiment I've done with a few fishing partners. I've been stream fishing with people who fancied themselves hotshot lake anglers, but were inexperienced on moving water. They insisted on using their lake-fishing techniques – and attributed their lack of success entirely to having the "wrong" lure. So I sweetly offered to switch lures with them. You know the results – they still continued to *not* catch fish and I still managed to do pretty well even with their less-than-perfect baits. The point is that lures are tools just like rods and reels, and using them properly is at least as important as selecting the right ones.

Now I'll talk about the six different categories of stream lures, and give you a few of my favorites of each type. A number of artificials made by specific manufacturers are also mentioned. These are baits I've used for a long time and are proven producers. However, there are usually other lures of the same category that also produce well. Some specific types of lures are made by over a dozen manufacturers, and almost all of them may be acceptable. So mentioning a certain model is not an endorsement of that one to the exclusion of others; it's simply the way I represent an entire category of artificials.

SPINNERS

Looking at North America as a whole, it's a safe bet to say that spinners of various sorts are still the most popular type of river smallmouth lures. Some of this popularity is simple tradition (spinners have been used on streams for decades), but it's also because these babies catch fish! I'm including in the spinner category almost all weighted and unweighted in-line spinners plus many safety-pin types. All these should be in the smaller (lighter) sizes: ¼ ounce or less, rarely up to ⅜ ounce.

Stream spinners should be able to be worked very slowly, be

Kneeling to become less visible to the fish is especially good on a small, clear stream. Here the author works an unweighted Cockatoush spinner through shallow water.

usable in very shallow water, and be workable around rocks, logs, and weeds. They should also allow you to work them deep and be highly visible or "noisy" when conditions call for it. No single spinner will do all these things perfectly, of course, but they should all do at least a couple of them. In-line spinners, especially, can be used for both active and less active fish.

Quickly working weighted spinners like Panther Martins or Mepps through the head of pool area or around rocks is a time-tested way to catch lots of active bass. But slowly and repeatedly working a spinner deep along the bottom of a pool will also take some of the less active "resting" fish. Surprisingly, unweighted in-line spinners (ones with light blades and unweighted spinner shafts) often work the best for deep and slow fishing. The actual lure itself is lightweight, but lead is attached on the line a foot or so ahead. Rigs like this are a little harder to cast but they enable you to retrieve slowly near bottom, with the spinner riding a little higher than the lead. Lightweight spinner-fly combinations can also be fished very shallow (with no lead) and kept in near-stationary positions against the current. Safety-pin spinners, either single or double bladed, are good around weeds and in low-visibility water. Stay away from the big "largemouth" models; ⅛ and ¼ ounce are the best sizes. Adding a ripple rind trailer to these baits often increases their effectiveness, especially in low-visibility water.

As experienced river fishermen know, one spinner in particular is in everybody's lure box. The Mepps has been slung into countless streams and lakes from Maine to Missouri for decades. This widespread use over many years has made the old Mepps number one in bass caught. Well, the Mepps is good, but it has weaknesses: it sinks too fast, the standard treble-hooked models hang up too easily, and it can't be retrieved extra slowly. A more snag-resistant model, the weedless Mepps Combo with a soft plastic tail on a single "keeper" hook, is better at avoiding hangups. To better set the hook, use 8-pound line with these "weedless" hooks.

Another oldie, the Cockatoush, has some strengths the Mepps doesn't. The Cockatoush spinner-fly is an unweighted in-line spinner with a large (and tantalizing) hackle fly attached. It can be fished very slowly and catches smallmouth, walleye, pickerel, and pike like crazy. Even though it was manufactured and sold for many years, it isn't currently being produced commercially. Fortu-

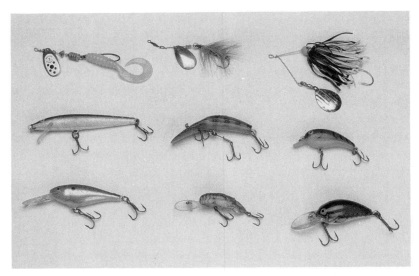

Some productive spinning lures. Spinners (top): Mepps Combo, Cockatoush spinner-fly, spinner bait. Shallow-running plugs: floating thin minnow, Flatfish, shallow-running crankbait. Medium-running crankbaits: Shad Rap, Rebel Crawfish crankbait, Bomber crankbait. Sheldon Bolstad.

nately, it's not too difficult to work up your own Cockatoush spinner-flies; see the end of this chapter for some tips on making your own. A good safety-pin spinner is a ⅛-ounce silver-bladed model made by Strike King. Adding a ripple rind to spinners of this sort increases their effectiveness.

SHALLOW-RUNNING PLUGS

In this category are a great many hard-bodied, minnow-imitating lures, mainly banana-shaped plugs and small-lipped, thin minnow types that either float at rest or are very slow sinkers. Those that float are the most versatile because they don't hang up as much. Any lures in this category should perform well in currents. Avoid plugs that have a tendency to run on their sides when they hit a slight cross current. And any plugs of this type should have good action when fished slowly.

Shallow-running plugs are primarily used to catch active smallmouth. Especially when bass are seen feeding on minnows near the surface or in the shallows, the thin minnow types are deadly. The old banana-shaped types like floating Lazy Ikes and Flatfish can also be used for less active fish. Clamping lead on the line will get these lures down so they can be slowly wobbled near the bottom. Even in today's era of high-tech baits, I still catch some good bass (and walleye) on the funny-looking Flatfish, especially the X-4 model. Some other entries in my hall of fame are the balsa wood Rapalas and Bagleys in sizes up to 5½ inches, and smaller-sized Rebel thin minnows. I have the best success with thin minnows that are either gold or silver sided.

These lures often run best with small snaps on them instead of being tied directly to the line. The problem is getting snaps that are small enough; big snaps or swivels can impair a lure's action and frighten wary fish in clear water. Very small split rings are okay, but are hard to take off a lure. "Fas Snaps" is one brand of tiny snap hooks that won't impair the action of even the smallest lures. They can be left on an individual lure, or you can leave them on the line and quickly take different lures on and off them with the aid of needle-nose pliers.

MEDIUM-RUNNING CRANKBAITS

This group includes a variety of crankbaits that float at rest and run from 4 to 8 feet deep. Stream crankbaits should be small or medium-sized. Those that run in a more vertical position—lip down, tail up—are the best at reducing hangups. And thin-bodied, high-vibration crankbaits (not the extra-fat types) seem to produce more stream bass.

Contrary to what many people believe, certain bottom-bumping crankbaits can be used in shallow waters. Used over sand, pebble, or smooth rock bottom, crankbaits can be fished in surprisingly shallow water. Even in only 2 feet of water, a crawfish-colored crankbait can be used so that it almost plows a furrow on a gravel or pebble bottom. This lure action probably reminds a bass of an escaping crawfish. Removing the belly hooks will help reduce bottom hangups. Just don't use a medium-running crankbait in areas with a lot of wood or broken rock.

Deep water, of course, is the specialty of this category. Getting a lure down through 5 feet of water in a moderate current is tough, except with crankbaits and jigs. During the warmer months, cranks that resemble crawfish do by far the best. Well-fed and finicky late summer bass, walleye, and channel catfish are often prodded into nailing high-vibration, bottom-bumping crankbaits.

Several years ago when Shad Rap fever was sweeping the area, I was a little skeptical of the feats attributed to it. But after using the Shad Rap for quite a while, I'm convinced it does indeed have a place in my lure box. This Rapala-made bait and similar crankbaits really can produce strikes from deeper or less active fish if conditions allow you to use it without hanging up excessively. Bomber's crawfish crankbait and Rebel's crawfish replicas are two other good producers in this category.

JIGS

This category includes a host of presentations that are basically a lead head molded on an upturned hook as their basic component, then dressed up in a variety of ways – feather, hair, pork, soft plastic, or tipped with live bait. Many anglers don't realize they can use jigs effectively on small rivers and even tiny creeks. In fact, on many small waters, lead heads are positively rare. Sure, shallow, rocky waters seem unlikely "habitat" for lead heads, but with the right jigs and a good technique you can jig fish in the tiniest creeks. The trick is going *light*. Throw out a ¼ or even ⅛ ounce of lead, and in many places you catch nothing but snags. But carefully work a ¹/₁₆-ounce or lighter jig, and you can fish and fish with few hangups.

General Jig Qualities and Use

Besides being as light as possible, what else should you look for in a stream jig? For one thing, slow sinking properties. You can make lead heads slow sinking by dressing them with lots of buoyant material. Small-headed jigs dressed with pork or plastic or even thick marabou feather all sink relatively slowly. For shallow water (less than 3 feet deep) a slow-sinking jig is essential. Fish also love to strike jigs that are slowly settling to the bottom. Speaking of strikes, small ($^1/16$ or $^1/32$ ounce) jigs often have hooks that are so small they make you miss many strikes. Avoid the ones with standard (small) hooks; number 2 or at least number 4 hooks are much better.

Also important is how well a jig avoids hooking unintended targets – snags. Actually, slow-sinking lead heads don't hang up much; faster-sinking ones are another matter. *Careful* use of lighter jigs is one way to cut down on hangups, but for extremely snag-ridden waters, snag guards are called for. The trouble is, most weed guards are also fish guards. Get commercial jigs with multiple-fiber guards and cut off individual strands until the guard is soft and flexible and you are left with a workable jig. This won't stop every snag, but it will eliminate most of them and it will allow you to hook fish even with a light rod and line. (See the end of the chapter for a way to make your own snag-guard–equipped jigs.)

The right weight and type of jig is only half the story. The other part is learning to use it properly. Most jigs probably remind bass of crawfish or bottom-dwelling minnows, so they should be fished near bottom. However, under most conditions dragging the jig right on the bottom isn't necessary. Instead, work the jig *near* bottom with very short hops or a slow pause-and-retrieve swimming motion, *not* any big lift-and-drop motions. It takes an attentive angler to maintain this action and detect light strikes.

Jigs can also be used as minnow-resembling baits (although other lures often do a better job of this). Tinsel or bucktail-dressed lead heads and many plastic single-tailed ones can be used as minnow imitators. These can all be fished a little faster and shallower than the crawfish imitators. If white bass also inhabit the streams you fish, having a couple of white or silver jigs along is almost mandatory.

Favorite Jigs

My favorite jigs in the "crawfish" category are double-tailed 2-inch plastic-bodied types, especially in yellow and purple (or motor oil for extra-clear water). Another good one is the Gapen Ugly Bug in brown or yellow. I've devised a vaguely similar jig with a chenille and hackle body and fewer rubber legs; I call it the Holschlag Hackle Jig. The old marabou-bodied jig ($^1/16$ or $^1/32$ ounce) is still quite good, especially in black and brown. A new jig on the scene that combines plastic and marabou is Cabela's Starburst. I have used this lure for only a season, but initial results are good. It is a very slow-sinking jig that stays in the standup position when it hits bottom.

Good minnow imitators are ¼- to ¹/₁₆-ounce tinsel jigs in silver and the 2½-inch white single-tailed plastic kinds. These are especially good in the spring, when crawfish are in short supply and minnows make up more of the bass's diet. Dozens of small companies make jigs and market them locally. If a local lead head looks good, don't be afraid to give it a try. You can also do what many others do to get just the right kind of jig for the conditions—make your own.

TOPWATERS

Topwaters are defined here as any baits that can be fished on the surface, even though they may also be used as subsurface lures. Various noisy and quiet baits are in the category, some of them so light and small they can also be cast with a fly rod.

Everybody loves to catch fish on the surface. It's great to watch the lure twitching, popping, or gurgling and then actually see the fish take it off the top, sometimes quietly, sometimes explosively. Not many river spin fishers think of using topwaters, but stream smallmouth can be caught very well on spinning-sized topwaters. During the spawn period and all through the summer season, river smallies love surface baits. In fact, smallmouth in very small creeks will probably strike on the surface more consistently than any species of bass under any other conditions.

Topwater Qualities and Use

The monstrosities commonly sold as topwater bass baits—huge things of ⅝ ounce or more—are not the way to go on rivers or creeks. You want smaller ones—¼ ounce or less, especially less. Baits that make a tremendous racket are also poor for stream smallmouth; those that make subdued popping or gurgling noises are much better, and sometimes those that make almost no noise are the best of all. The size and shape of a topwater also determines its hooking ability. Larger, thicker-bodied surface plugs do not hook smallmouth very well. Those with small hooks don't allow consistent hooking, so replace these short-shanked (and probably dull) hooks with longer-shanked wire treble hooks honed very sharp.

Surface lures in moving water tend to move when you don't want them to, as they drift away in the current. You can overcome this by casting only to calmer water or by casting from upstream and working the lure against the current. Repeatedly popping or "chugging" the lure in the same place by pulling it against the current sometimes works wonders.

Early mornings and evenings are normally the most consistent times to catch smallies on topwaters. But I've also seen many hot, bright afternoons when the fish positively destroyed surface baits. So don't be afraid to try topwaters at any time of the day. Fifteen minutes will tell you if the bass are interested. And no matter what the time of day, casting close to the bank is the best method. When using surface baits, drop them *quietly* onto the surface; muskies, pike, even the largemouth may like a loud *kersplash,* but the cautious smallie doesn't. Also keep in mind that bass in very small streams are very surface oriented, probably because in these shallow and narrow creeks they are always so close to the surface and the banks. Whatever the reason, little creeks and hot surface action go together.

To give you some idea of how effective surface fishing can be, let me recount a recent experience. One evening my partner and I were fishing a small pasture stream. I was fishing the water first and he was following right behind me. In 400 yards of stream I caught six bass, all under 13 inches. Fishing the *same places* right behind me, my buddy caught and released seven bass, including two dandies, over 16 inches. I pounded this water with various subsurface baits; he used only a surface lure.

Topwater Picks

Here are some good topwaters. Heddon's extra small Hula Popper is fine; trim the rubber skirt to make it shorter and narrower. Another Heddon product is also good – a heavy, hard plastic fly-rod popper. It weighs $1/16$ ounce and can be cast 30 or 40 feet. The rubber skirt on

More spinning lures. Topwaters (top): Propeller topwater, Heddon spinning popper. Jigs: double-tailed plastic jig, single-tailed plastic jig, silver tinsel jig. "Soft, light and little" baits: ¹/₃₂-ounce marabou jig, unweighted pork eel, small Rebel thin minnow. Sheldon Bolstad.

this one should also be trimmed. The immobile single hook is excellent for hooking even 10-inchers. A good propeller bait is the Tiny Torpedo.

Other good surface baits that aren't even "official" topwaters are balsa thin minnows about 3½ inches long. I've caught tons of smallies on the surface with Rapalas and other floating thin minnows. This is a quiet lure that should be just "jiggled" in place without actually moving it. A topwater good for larger fish is the Hubs Chub Rattalur. This is a popular Mid-South smallmouth lure not widely used in other regions. It's a little noisier and larger than most of my other topwaters, but is quite good for larger-sized bass.

"SOFT, LIGHT, AND LITTLE" BAITS

In this group several different types are lumped together. The main thing they have in common is their ability to catch smallmouth under very difficult conditions, like ultraclear or cold water, or when the fish are extra finicky for whatever reason. Included in the category are tiny plugs and spinners, ultralight jigs, soft and natural-feel jigs, and extra-soft, small plastic worms. They are specialized in the sense that they aren't really needed for normal situations; they come in handy maybe 15 percent of the time. Some instances where soft, light, and little baits really pay off are in very clear streams or when bass are on their beds in very shallow water.

To make use of their potential, you need some extra finesse for almost all these baits. This means you must be able to use very light lines, work a nearly weightless lure extremely slowly in the current, and detect almost imperceptible strikes. The lures in this group are best left to the more experienced. The major exception is the live-bait–tipped lead head, which can be used successfully with only a little practice.

Here are several you may want to consider.

Rebel 1½-inch thin minnows – Baby Bass imitations or gold-sided models (the factory hooks may be too small to hook and hold bass, so replace them with larger ones).

1/32-ounce marabou jigs – with extra marabou, tied on a number 2 jig hook in brown or black, and used on a 2-pound test line.

Brown pork crawdads – 2¾-inch size on a 1/16-ounce sparsely dressed brown marabou jig. The jig hook must be at least size 1. A little commercial crawfish scent sometimes helps.

Unweighted black pork eels – on a short-shank number 4 hook.

Nymph patterns – tied on a 1/32-ounce lead head. It's hard to find these commercially made; check with good trout shops, or tie them yourself.

Minnows or crawfish on ⅛- to 1/32-ounce short-shanked jigs – hook the minnow through the lips and try a red-colored jig head. Any crawfish used should be about 2 inches long and should be hooked through the tail so it can be retrieved backward. The jig and minnow combo is good in the very cold waters of early spring or late fall.

Panfish-sized curly-tailed soft plastic jigs – especially black ones on 1/32-ounce heads.

LURE COLOR

Reflecting on many years of stream fishing, I've noticed that a few color patterns emerge. Try my recommended color schemes first, but if they don't pay off don't hesitate to experiment a little.

From early spring to early summer, lures with lots of white, silver, or other bright colors are best: silver-sided thin minnows, silver-bladed spinners, and white and chartreuse jigs. During this time, crawfish haven't yet emerged and small fish make up significant portions of the bass's diet. Also, the water clarity is not normally very good during this time. Starting in early or midsummer until the end of the year, baits with gold, brown, black, and crawfish orange are good. This means things like gold spinner blades and crawfish color patterns. For rivers that have *naturally* dark-stained water, like those with considerable bog drainage, both high-visibility colors and dark colors like black work well.

ARTIFICIALS VERSUS LIVE BAIT

I have deliberately omitted specific information on live bait. As I said before, a catch-and-release philosophy is crucial in our efforts to maintain quality smallmouth fishing. With careful use of artificials, nearly all bass caught and released will live. On the other hand, *still fishing* with live bait causes mortal injuries to a significant number of the fish caught. So I cannot in good conscience promote live-bait

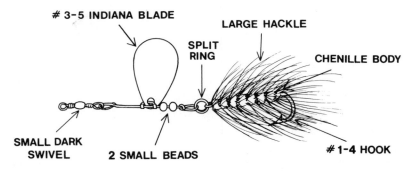

Cockatoush spinner-fly. The large tantalizing fly is one of the Cockatoush's important features. Building a small dark-colored swivel into this spinner eliminates line twist.

use. Please read the final chapter carefully for more information about preserving our fishing resources.

However, this doesn't exclude the practice of "tipping" artificials. Putting a piece of natural bait or a whole minnow on a *retrieved* artificial, like a jig or spinner, causes no higher fish mortality than "plain" artificials. And don't forget, plain or tipped artificials will very often outfish live bait by a wide margin. Learning to use lures skillfully isn't difficult; you will increase your catches, and the fish will live to fight again and again.

MAKING SMALLMOUTH LURES

Cockatoush Spinner-Flies

As I mentioned previously, the Cockatoush can be a very effective lure. Because it's an unweighted spinner it can easily be coaxed through extremely shallow water. Weed-guard–equipped, it can be slowly and effectively fished around logs and aquatic vegetation. And with generous amounts of lead attached, this lightweight spinner can also be used in deeper water, if the current isn't too strong. The Cockatoush was developed many decades ago, and gained a dedicated following of highly experienced anglers before it ceased being sold commercially some years back. In fact, bass fishing legend Jason Lucas, longtime angling editor of *Sports Afield* magazine, noted way back in the 1940s: "One of the favorite lures of all really advanced and expert bass fishermen whom I know is a fly and spinner, with a small lead weight to carry them out."

Well, Jason Lucas is gone and the venerable Cockatoush is no longer in the tackle shops, but you can still make use of its talents if you make your own. The easiest part is the spinner itself. You can obtain Indiana spinners in sizes 3 to 5 already mounted on short spinner shafts from many tackle shops. Or you can easily assemble them from scratch by purchasing the blades, clevises, split rings, plastic beads, and wire shaft material individually. Be sure to build in a small swivel to avoid line twists. Depending on water conditions and food sources, use brass or silver-colored blades; the newer, more exotic blade colors such as fluorescent orange or chartreuse don't seem to produce as often.

A good fly to go with the spinner is important. The old commercial Cockatoush flies were often very large flies tied on long-shank 2/0 hooks, and made with large amounts of chenille and large hen hackles. Flies that large are seldom necessary (number 1 or 2 hooks are fine), but the chenille and hackle bodies are essential. If you don't want to tie your own flies, you can buy reverse hackle-flies that are adequate substitutes. Tying a loop of heavy monofilament into the fly is a good way to make it almost snagless. Just remember that even a very flexible guard will also deflect a few fish strikes. Numerous fly colors are good, but a plain light brown is consistently the best.

Holschlag Hackle Jig

Jigs with a set of rubber legs sometimes produce when few others interest the fish. Precisely why this is so only the fish know for sure, but it's probably because these lures have such tantalizing action with those legs waving about. A few years ago I decided to add a feather and chenille body to a rubber-legged jig. The result was a jig with a much fuzzier look than the smooth plastic-bodied jigs sold commercially. This fuzzy look seems to add to the jig's allure, since it catches fish very well.

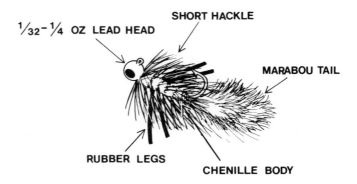

Holschlag hackle jig. Along with the flexible rubber legs, the hackle and chenille body give this jig a fuzzy, undulating look. Tied on a ¹/₃₂-ounce lead head, this lure can also be used with fly tackle.

A fly tier or jig maker can produce these jigs at home. Round jig heads are fine. Besides thread and head cement, you'll need marabou for the tail (brown is good), thin "rubber band" legs (white or yellow both work), and chenille (brown, yellow, and black are favorites). First attach the tail, then wrap the chenille body, then attach the legs. Finally, wrap a fly hackle around the body (from head to tail) to finish the jig. You can paint the jig head either first or last. The completed jig probably doesn't closely imitate any particular food source, but it seems to appear quite tantalizing to the fish. When equipped with a weed (snag) guard, these rubber-legged jigs are good at probing rocky or log-filled areas.

Snag-Resistant Jigs

Too often jigs (and other lures) equipped with commercially made guards to prevent snagging also prevent hooking fish. The wire or fiber guards commercially used are usually too stiff; it takes a rod like a pool cue to hook many fish on these guards. One way to obtain more flexible guards is to make your own out of heavy monofilament. Using a small drill bit, drill a hole into the jig head. Make sure the angle of the hole allows the mono guards to align right above the hook point. Next cut six sections of 20-pound mono, each at least 1 inch long. Insert them into the drilled hole along with plenty of thick waterproof epoxy. After the epoxy has dried you can trim the heavy mono strands to the desired length and paint the jig head. These guards won't prevent every hangup, but will eliminate most of them; most important, they will allow you to use a regular stream rod and still be able to hook fish.

10 ～

Fly Fishing for Stream Smallmouth

FLY FISHING IS OFTEN DESCRIBED as "the ultimate challenge," and it is – but it's also a good way to catch lots of fish! Don't be hoodwinked by the mystique that surrounds fly fishing. It's not an elite sport or some kind of stunt. Not at all. Besides being an absolutely exciting and enjoyable way to fish, fly fishing is also practical and relatively simple to do. If you have never fished with the fly rod, do think about trying it. And I especially want to encourage those who use their long rods only for trout to give "river bass" a try. Once you start latching onto some rod-bending, high-jumping stream smallmouth, your trout fishing may well be put on the back burner.

If you are willing to gather the appropriate tackle and spend a few hours learning to cast, you can start catching fish on a fly rod shortly after hitting the stream. And finding good waters isn't hard. Well over three-quarters of our smallmouth waterways are big or open enough to allow easy casting. But even the narrowest and brushiest creeks can be fished by experienced fly fishers. Even fish species rarely taken on fly tackle, like walleye or channel catfish, can be easily caught on flies in smaller rivers or creeks. It's not hard to take walleye on a fly rod out of a small 4-foot pool. And then there is the excitement of the fight. Even a 14-inch smallmouth is awesome on a 5-weight rod. Hooking larger fish, say 17 or 18 inches, must be experienced to be fully appreciated.

Fly fishing is a challenging and exciting way to fish for smallmouth.

Another advantage of fly fishing is that you can use lightweight lures. At times, small, lightweight surface or subsurface flies are some of the most effective bait you can use. For example, cork poppers are dynamite for stream bass and really can't be cast with anything but fly tackle. Finally, there is the special pleasure of the casting itself. Sure, making precision casts with a spin stick is enjoyable, but it just can't match the satisfaction you feel when your fly casting becomes good.

LEARNING TO FLY FISH FOR SMALLMOUTH

Learning to lay out a decent cast with the fly rod is obviously not as easy as picking up a spinning stick and throwing out a ⅛-ounce lead head. You need three or four short practice sessions with the fly rod, so you can learn to easily cast 40 feet (far enough for starters). The assistance of an experienced fly fisher is very helpful in learning to cast, but isn't absolutely necessary. If you are reasonably coordinated and diligent, you can learn on your own with the help of how-to books or videos.

Be aware that there are a few streams or sections of streams that are tough fishing with fly tackle. Extremely narrow waters with lots of overhanging trees can cause even the best casters headaches with their back casts. Fortunately, there are plenty of other places to fish. Wind can also be a headache for the fly fisher. Strong winds (over 20 miles per hour) make casting tough, but you can minimize this problem by staying on smaller, protected waters on windy days.

Another limitation of fly fishing is the type of baits you can throw; there are no big crankbaits, spinner baits, or jigs in the fly fisher's lure box. But even this isn't as limiting as most people assume. The fly rodder doesn't have to stick with just small and lightweight flies. Purists may protest, but some of the smaller and lighter "spinning" lures can be used with little trouble. I use very small ($1/32$-ounce) jigs and small spinner-flies even with my 5-weight outfit.

As you're getting started, the assistance of a friend or tackle shop clerk knowledgeable in *smallmouth* fishing is invaluable. Unfortunately, some shop advice is better suited to trout fishing or is heavily slanted toward selling you their most costly items. If possible, try several places to get different opinions. Books, magazines, and the new fly-fishing videos are also good sources of advice on tackle, casting, and techniques.

If you come to bass fishing from trout fishing, you'll need to make a few adjustments. For instance, many trout fishers can make good delicate presentations but can't cast very far. Learn to increase your casting to at least 55 feet. Getting comfortable casting larger, heavier flies can also take time. Many trout anglers also have trouble solidly setting the hook on smallmouth. Remember, the bass's mouth is a lot harder than a trout's and your leader is probably heavier. Don't be afraid to sock it to 'em.

TACKLE TIPS

First of all, you *don't* need the heavy-duty stuff often called "bass bugging" outfits. These heavy rods and lines (8-weight or more) may be needed for bigmouth on some lakes, but they aren't needed or desirable for most streams.

Rods

To obtain the most enjoyment from your fishing, go with a 6-weight, 8½- or 9-foot rod. Even a 5-weight rod in the same length is adequate for some situations. A 15-inch smallie on a 6-weight rod will positively wear you out and make you a confirmed light-tackle enthusiast. An outfit of this weight won't allow you to lay out 90-foot casts with big deer-hair bugs, but more modest-sized poppers, streamers, and nymphs cast fine. If you're a trout angler with only a 5-weight outfit and don't want to rush out and buy a new rod, try your light rod for a while. Stay out of the wind and stick with the smaller, easier-to-cast flies.

The rod that will give you the most trouble is one with an extra-delicate (flexible) tip. "Trout rods" of this type make it hard to cast the larger bass flies you will use. Strong rod tips are much better to lift your flies off the water. If you plan to use large, bulky flies on big, wide-open rivers, then a 7-weight rod is in order. An 8½-foot 7-weight will allow you to handle bulky flies and wind much better than the lighter outfits can. But it's a little more tiring to use for everyday fishing and it won't produce quite as much fight from every fish as lighter sticks do.

You can spend anywhere from $50 to $400 for a good rod. For those just starting out, a $50 to $75 graphite rod is fine. Some will disagree (such as clerks in high-priced fly shops), but I don't think the extremely expensive models are significantly better than more moderately priced ($100) rods. My basic view on tackle and equipment costs is that fly fishers as a group spend too much and spin fishers spend too little.

Lines

Choosing the right fly line is easy nowadays. Simply get a good quality line that matches the rating on your rod, make sure it's a floating weight-forward or bass-bug taper, and you can hardly go wrong. Bass-bug tapers are sort of extra weight-forward lines and work well to cast bulky flies like deer-hair "bugs." To more easily cast longer distances with less bulky flies, use the regular weight-forward line. For the shallower waters typical of most small and mid-sized streams, you'll only rarely need sinking lines. For deeper rivers, you will occasionally find a sinking line valuable in getting and keeping the fly down, but even there a Sink-Tip line is preferred over a full sinking line. For those just starting out, I recommend sticking with a full floating line.

No matter what line you use, regular cleaning and dressing will prolong its life and make your casting significantly easier. About 80 feet is all you need for most situations. I know some people like to recommend (or even insist) that every fly reel be loaded with immense quantities of line and backing. But I say, just make sure your particular reel is filled properly and don't worry about having lots of reserve backing (unless your streams also contain 30-pound salmon).

Reels

My views on lines also influence my ideas on reels. Since large amounts of line or backing aren't necessary, reels with extra-large line capacities aren't either. I also don't believe the reel's drag is very important since it's rarely needed while fishing. What you *do* need is a single-action reel you can operate with your opposite hand. Get a left-handed reel if you are right-handed; this saves you from having to shift your rod from one hand to the other. A reel that allows spools to be interchanged is also nice. If you can quickly replace your double-taper trout line with a spool of weight-forward bass line, you can make the reel do double duty. Automatic reels are very heavy and don't allow interchangeability of spools. If you don't already have an automatic, don't get one. As of this writing, $40 will still buy a practical and decent-quality fly reel. You may want to spend $20 or $30 more, but shelling out a small fortune for a good reel won't be necessary.

Leaders

Leaders that will perform well are important. Follow a few simple rules and you shouldn't have any problems. Fortunately, extra-long leaders (over 10 feet) or extra-light ones (tippets of 3-pound test or less) aren't needed. Tapered leaders 8½ feet long with tippets from

4 to 8 pounds are good. Anything longer than this is needed only in very clear water conditions where the fish are extra skittish. Even then, a 10-footer will be enough. Besides being easier to lay out properly, an 8½-footer is short enough so the line to leader knot won't hang up in the guides of 9-foot rods.

Tapered leaders, either commercial or homemade, should more or less follow the 60–20–20 formula: a 60 percent heavy butt section, a 20 percent intermediate "step-down" section, and a 20 percent tippet. Several companies make good leaders for about $1. One company markets butt-section leader material called Amnesia in a bright fluorescent color. Leaders with this highly visible butt section are nice for fishing subsurface flies. Being able to easily see the first few feet of the leader aids in strike detection.

One problem on all leaders is that the tippet section quickly gets short if you fish a lot or change flies a lot. The way to easily and cheaply solve this is to get a short, heavy leader like a 7½-foot 0X and tie your own 18- to 24-inch tippet on it. This extra material can be regular monofilament. After you tie the leader to the line and put a loop on the other end, the "heavy" leader portion will be about 7 feet. When the extra 18 to 24 inches of tippet is added, you have a leader of just the right length. More important, when the tippet becomes too short another section can quickly be tied to the loop, so you avoid having to frequently replace the entire leader. And as experienced fly rodders know, fine leaders can also be made from scratch. Also, if the water visibility is low and you don't care whether the leader lies out straight, a 7-foot length of 8-pound mono will do.

Knots and Strike Indicators

Knots are needed to link the line and leader, sometimes to put a loop in the leader, and to tie on flies. What knots are best for these jobs? Actually it isn't difficult. If you learn to tie the double surgeon's loop, the double surgeon's knot, and the uni knot, that should eliminate most knot problems. Companies that manufacture lines and leaders generally enclose a handy illustrated booklet on knots.

Another challenge faced by fly fishers is detecting strikes

when fishing below the surface, especially when drifting or retrieving with the current. Strike indicators that can be stuck on the line or leader are good in helping to detect these slack-line strikes. Many people like the soft, bright-colored indicators that you can slide up and down the leader. They can't be reused, but a pack of two dozen will last a long time.

FLIES AND LURES

More than traditional flies can be used with the fly rod. Tiny jigs and spinners cast tolerably well and are very effective additions to your poppers, streamers, and such. Starting on the surface and going down toward the bottom, let's see what should be included in a fly fisher's bag of tricks.

Topwaters

Various types of topwater poppers and surface bugs are very effective for stream fishing, and not just for smallmouth; several sunfish species, mooneye, and even members of the esox (pike) family also fall for topwaters. As a general rule, smaller ones produce the most strikes. My favorites are smaller cork-bodied poppers. Painting the backs fluorescent orange helps significantly in seeing them under poor light conditions. When small sunfish are extremely thick and are climbing all over your small popper, you may want to switch to bigger topwaters for bass. Deer-hair bugs can be a little hard to throw with light rods but they do bring the fish up to the top. A good one is the Dahlberg Diver. This topwater, as its name implies, can also double as a subsurface bait when it's retrieved rapidly. The Dahlberg Diver is best on the surface but will take plenty of fish underwater too. It's also one surface bait that is better in the larger sizes (number 1 or 2 hook).

Some of the most exciting surface fishing takes place where smallmouth actively feed on insect hatches, just like trout. In some areas, like Virginia, there are heavy caddis, brown drake, and stonefly hatches on smallmouth streams. If good hatches of large-sized insects occur on your area streams (and the bass are used to

Fly fisher Sheldon Bolstad with a fine summer evening catch taken on a topwater popper.

feeding on them), it will pay to carry some of these dry-fly imitations. No matter what pattern, the larger sizes – number 10, 8, or larger – are best.

Streamers

In the streamer category, dozens of patterns will produce. Seeing what the local fly shops sell a lot of may narrow down the choices. One standby of many good anglers is a simple marabou streamer. Black and white are favorite marabou colors; yellow and olive are next. The famous Muddler Minnows are also good most places, although they aren't as easy to cast as marabou streamers. For moving-water fishing a fur-headed Muddler is best; the fur-headed versions sink better than the standard deer-hair patterns. The Woolly Bugger, another old standby, is perhaps the most important fly to have in your vest. A fly of this type about 2½ inches long is truly an excellent producer and can be cast easily by even very light outfits. Be sure to carry some in brown, black, yellow, and white.

Woolly Buggers can be used very effectively near the bottom, but sculpin and leech patterns are also good for bottom work. When the bass are particularly inactive, sculpin patterns like the Spuddler will usually rustle up a little action.

I'm also including in the streamer category unweighted spinner-flies. They are not the most pleasant things to throw around, but modest distances are possible and spinner-flies are great fish catchers. Even standard streamer patterns on a small Indiana spinner are often good. My favorite is a small brown Cockatoush fly on a small brass blade. Fish these much like you would regular streamers, but be prepared for a raised eyebrow or two if you decide to tie on a little spinner-fly or small jig in the presence of a fly-fishing purist.

Nymph Patterns

In the last category are weighted nymphs or nymphlike lures. Check in your area to see if there are any local favorites. Small-mouth-sized nymphs should be larger than many of the tiny ones commonly used for trout; sizes 2 to 6 are much better. Weighted stonefly and hellgrammite nymphs are two popular patterns. Some other effective nymphlike "flies" are those tied on small lead heads ($1/32$ ounce). The pattern isn't critical, but those in browns, blacks, and grays and with tails are best. The lead in the head gives this lure a more enticing "jigging" action than conventional nymphs with their weight in the body.

Don't let yourself get hooked by some of those intricate crawfish imitations that look pretty in the box but are lightweight, hard, stiff, and perform poorly. One simpler but much more effective crawfish pattern is the Squirrel Tail Crawfish. It's mostly a weighed brown chenille body with squirrel tail pincers, but it catches fish.

BASIC TECHNIQUES

Many of the techniques and concepts described in earlier chapters can and should be used by the fly fisher. Remember, the fish and its

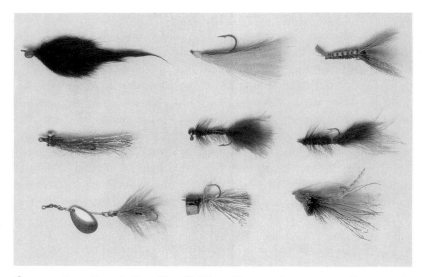

Some good smallmouth flies. Top: Dahlberg Diver, cork popper, small spinner-fly. Middle: Woolly Bugger, Lead Headed Woolly Bugger, Clouser minnow. Bottom: squirrel-tail crawfish, marabou streamer, leech.

reactions to its environment don't change just because your rod is longer than the one spin fishers use. The basic methods described here are largely modifications of the other techniques explained in this book.

Surface Fishing

The most enjoyable, and often the easiest, way to fly fish for smallmouth is to take them on top. Stream bass can be caught on the surface from late spring to early fall. And the smaller the stream, the more surface oriented the fish. On small creeks, surface poppers and bugs catch smallmouth like crazy. So don't hesitate to try topwaters any time of the day. After twenty minutes or so, switch to subsurface stuff if there is no response on the top.

The conventional manner of fishing topwaters on larger floatable waters is bank shooting. One person controls the craft's drift parallel to the targeted bank while the other person fishes, dropping casts just inches from the bank. Under the right conditions this is deadly. For the on-foot angler, the most common way to fish topwaters is to cast across and upstream toward the banks. If the current isn't too strong this is a good tactic. Be prepared for strikes as soon as the lure hits the water. If no takes occur immediately, rest the lure a few seconds and then give it three or four pops or twitches interspersed with pauses.

If the current is strong enough to sweep the lure away quickly, it's best to use the upstream approach. Very cautiously, sneak into position *upstream* of your targeted area. From this position you can keep the lure from drifting away. At times, the fish will only take a popper held nearly stationary in the current. Give it a pop every few seconds while it remains almost in the same place. After twenty or thirty seconds, after you've nearly given up hope of a strike, old Red Eye may still come charging up.

Streamer and Spinner-Fly Fishing

Traditional streamer flies and lightweight spinner-flies can be fished in various ways. Streamers are effective retrieved with the current, against the current, or across stream. The main problem most people have when they try to fish a streamer (or spinner-fly) with the current is keeping a tight line. Some get very proficient in rapidly stripping in line as they bring a streamer back, but for most who are newer to the sport this is a tough way to fish. An easier way is to work streamers across and against the current. This way the current will both give the fly more lifelike action and keep tension on the line. Sneaking up to the head of the pool and working this area with a short line is very effective. In fact, I'd recommend that newer fly fishers fish *against* the current as their primary angling method for several months.

Slowly, thoroughly, and cautiously fish the heads of pools (including side eddies), boulders, logs, undercuts – any fish-holding areas you can work with a short, tight line. I like to keep moving, but when I do stop and work small areas thoroughly my catch rate goes up. Besides, working a fly on 20 feet of line right in front of you is a good way to learn to handle the rod, line, and lure and to hook fish.

Nymph Fishing

This includes any fishing that entails bringing the lure back slow and deep with the current. "Nymphing" is more difficult than surface or even mid-depth, tight-line streamer fishing. If you're new to fly fishing, stick with the easier techniques for at least several trips. When you have moderate proficiency with these other techniques, give nymphing a try.

Start in places where a short line will be adequate (30 feet is plenty), and avoid areas with stiff currents. Nobody enjoys trying to contend with long lines or strong currents. With only 30 feet or less of line out you should be able to see your strike indicator well enough to detect most hits. Put the indicator far enough above the lure so it isn't pulled too far under the surface by the weight of the lure. Experiment a little until you find the best placement for the indicator; try two a couple of feet apart if one isn't enough.

It should be obvious that this type of angling requires your full attention. One way to cut down on the strain of having to concentrate so intently is to switch to streamer or surface fishing every forty-five minutes. Of course, if the fish are hitting like mad, you probably won't notice any strain.

Small lead heads will at times do better than conventionally tied nymphs. Sure, you can clamp lead on the leader near the eye of regular nymphs, but flies weighted this way are poor substitutes for the old reliable molded lead head, where the hook also points up, avoiding hangups. Various dark-colored nymph patterns tied on $1/32$-ounce lead heads and extra-large hooks (at least size 4) work very well.

Canoes and Fly Fishing

Fly rodding from a canoe or other watercraft can be as productive as it is for the spin fisher, and the basic rules of floating also apply. The most popular way to fish from a stream craft is to bank shoot (see the float-fishing chapter). This method is both easy and productive, since it allows you to establish an easy cast-and-retrieve rhythm and cover lots of water.

There are a couple of small problems you will have to deal

with: how to avoid hitting your partner with the backcast, and what to do with your loose line. The backcast problem can be solved easily if only the person in the bow fishes, and only out of one side of the craft. Anglers should periodically switch roles so both get an opportunity to fish. Loose line in a canoe can turn into real aggravation. Repeatedly catching the line on various objects in the craft or stepping on it messes up your casts and can even damage the line. Before starting to fish, clear out the area around your feet, then avoid shuffling your feet while fishing. Casting while sitting in a canoe can be a little awkward at first; it's best to become a reasonably proficient on-foot caster first.

11 ~~~

Catching Big Smallmouth

ALMOST EVERYONE DREAMS of catching a really *big* fish. River smallmouth anglers are doubly blessed; not only are "trophy" stream bass available in many waters, but big smallies are unquestionably outstanding fish. While many species become slower and more sluggish with greater size, not the mighty smallmouth. As the smallmouth's size and weight increase so do its strength, speed, and jumping capability. No one ever gets bored catching big smallies!

That's what this chapter is all about—catching big smallmouth. But I'm not going to tell you a "secret" technique that will guarantee big fish every time out. Rather, I am going to give you several basic tips that will definitely increase your *chances* of catching big bass. Also, let's agree on what makes a "big" smallmouth. In almost all the intermediate to small rivers across the continent, a smallmouth of 4 to 4½ pounds (20 inches or more) is truly a big bass; anything much larger is rare. In fact, a 3-pound bass (17 inches or more) is truly a trophy in many small creeks, especially ones that don't have much deep water. Even the largest rivers don't see many smallies over 4 pounds. The overall numbers of big fish are also low in most waters. In even the best rivers, 4-pounders make up only a very small percentage of the overall bass population. Claims of hordes of huge smallmouth mostly come from people who never actually weigh their fish or from people trying to sell you something (like fishing magazines or fishing trips to their resorts). The bottom line is this: stream bass over 3 pounds are extremely fine fish and 4-pounders are absolute giants, and should be regarded as such.

BEST PLACES FOR BIG BASS

In every area, certain streams are better at producing large fish. Often they are the larger rivers, but even certain smaller waters consistently produce more lunker smallmouth than other streams. These "big-bass waters" fall into two general categories: rivers with exceptional fertility and habitat conditions, and streams that support only a few big fish but receive very little fishing pressure.

High-Fertility Waters

High fertility means lots of smallmouth food and high growth rates. These waters have good reproduction and plenty of big-bass habitat (areas in the stream with deep water and good cover). But these environmental conditions don't automatically guarantee big bass. If the stream receives heavy catch-and-kill pressure, it won't have many big smallmouth no matter how fertile. The streams to look for are those with high fertility but only moderate fishing pressure.

Big-fish rivers of this type are often fairly easy to find. Start by calling the appropriate fisheries department. Sometimes finding out what years had high bass reproduction will help you determine when a lot of fish will reach the lunker category in a particular stream. (It normally takes six to eight years for river smallmouth to grow to over 18 inches.) Regional fish managers are the best sources of information on reproductive success. Inquiries at local river-oriented tackle shops can also produce good information. No matter what the source, make sure the information you get is as current as possible. Just because a river had big fish four or five years ago doesn't mean it still has them. If catch-and-kill angling has recently increased on a particular stream, the number of big fish has probably declined. Obviously, a stream with regulations that protect the bigger fish would be the best bet for consistent success.

Lightly Fished Waters

If they receive little fishing pressure, even streams without high growth rates or high numbers of bigger fish will give you good chances of catching big bass. The smallmouth fishery in these waters is very fragile, in the sense that even moderate amounts of catch-and-kill fishing would quickly ruin the angling. The big bass in these waters exist primarily because few people fish for them. And these waters don't necessarily have to be large. I know many "secret" streams or sections that are barely able to be floated by canoe but still hold some very fine fish. Of course, finding this type of stream isn't as easy as finding more popular waters. State fisheries departments may not know much about them and tackle shops will probably also be in the dark. And if there are any local anglers that know their secrets, they're probably keeping quiet.

FINDING BIG-BASS WATERS

So how to find these "secret" hotspots? Work for them! Use some of the same methods described in the chapter on finding little-known streams. Sift through any written material you can, both fisheries commission reports and magazine and newspaper articles. Ask lots of questions. Take special note if several sources mention a specific stream. Get out the maps; look for streams that are less accessible than others.

After this homework, head for your targeted waters. Focus your attention on the sections of river that seem the most inaccessible or overlooked, as long as they have *some* big-fish habitat (water at least 4 or 5 feet deep with cover). As a general rule, the clearer the water, the deeper the water required to hold big fish. Streams too small to float with extremely thick, brushy banks are one type of inaccessible water, and so are streams with lots of downed trees blocking the channel. Quiet stretches of waterway between whitewater areas are another type. One of the most overlooked big-bass areas occurs in rivers that seem to have almost no smallmouth habitat. Some streams (say sandy bottomed or marshy) that are not thought of as smallmouth water often have isolated stretches with proper gradients, good rocky substrate, and adequate depths. These

This 3-pound smallmouth was taken from an overlooked wood-filled stream using the Holschlag hackle jig. Lyn Verthein.

overlooked stretches can have some real lunkers, simply because no one knows about them. For instance, I once took a 4¾-pound lunker from a small, predominantly marshy stream that few people are aware even supports smallmouth. While floating this stream I discovered an isolated stretch of good bass habitat among several miles of marshy stream. This small amount of stream couldn't support many bass, but since it was so lightly fished some of those that were present could attain lunker proportions.

Big-Fish Spots in a Stream

How do you find the best big-fish spots in a specific stream? Just heading out and fishing anywhere and everywhere will produce only the occasional big fish. If you really want to catch more than your share, spend as much of your fishing time as possible over big-fish holding areas.

After spawning, most river bass move into areas where they will spend at least the next several months. On a small creek, that may be a tiny pool only a few yards long. For bigger waters, it may be a stretch 200 yards long. And unless river conditions change dramatically, the smallmouth will stick close to these relatively small areas where they have adequate food, cover, and resting (holding) habitat. Larger fish seek out areas that can provide these essentials; smaller fish take the less desirable spots.

In a typical stream, these "best areas" are pools with some water at least 4 to 5 feet deep and good rock or wood cover. However, in very clear water (where it's easy for you to see the bottom) large fish will seldom take up residence in a spot only 4 or 5 feet deep, unless there is a large amount of wood cover, like a thick tree root system in an undercut bank. For big fish to feel safe in an open pool in clear water, they need at least 6 or 7 feet of water over their heads. Big fish certainly don't spend all their time in deep water, but without ready access to deep water and good cover an area seldom holds a significant number of big bass.

In smaller and shallower streams, big-bass areas are pretty easy to find. Often only one or two pools per mile have the depth and cover necessary to consistently attract the biggest fish. In larger waters, the big-bass hotspots may not be so obvious, since many

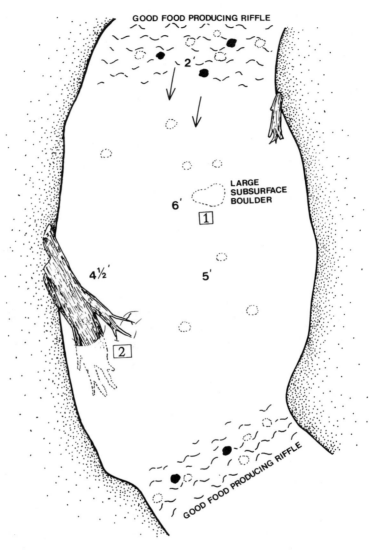

This pool has the ingredients for supporting big smallmouth: deep-water cover and easy access to food-producing areas. Position 1 behind a large deep-water boulder is a prime holding area for the biggest fish. Position 2 around a large log is also an excellent lunker spot.

pools or glides may have good cover in deep water. However, even here an observant angler can still key in on the best areas. By carefully observing a mile or more of river (depending on whether you are on foot or floating) you can see which are the very best-looking areas.

Overall, perhaps the best places to find big fish (and the places most overlooked by anglers) are near large underwater rocks in deep water. If the rocks are at least 3 feet in diameter they can create a calm-water holding area large enough to attract bigger fish. You can almost always detect these deep-water boulders by a telltale surface disturbance, however slight. In more heavily fished waters, rocks that are far below the surface and aren't easily detected produce the most big fish. Even a large rock or cluster of rocks in fairly strong currents can act as a big fish-holding area if it creates a large enough eddy. Sometimes you can determine the dimensions of an invisible rock and the force of the current behind it by carefully observing your line as the lure passes over and past the rock.

Certain types of wood cover also attract and hold big smallmouth. Large logs in water at least 4 feet deep are excellent places to look for lunkers. The best logs are those that have been in the same place for at least a year and still have some large branches on them. Logs sitting in areas with moderate to heavy current don't attract big fish. Look for downed trees in slow-current areas. Big logs resting up against deep-water banks are favored places.

During the relatively short spawn period, big bass are in different haunts. Like all sexually mature bass, they seek out areas suitable for spawning. You should know that the best fish take the best spawning sites, so by targeting these sites you can be fishing over the biggest fish. The best spawning sites are those that are well shielded from strong current flows and also have some nearby cover. Large logs and boulders accomplish both needs. Boulders several feet in diameter in 3 to 5 feet of water are very good big-fish spawning areas. Naturally, the fish build their bed on the downstream side of the boulder so it is protected from strong currents. Smaller bass often spawn in water shallower than 3 feet, but the very biggest fish like somewhat deeper water if it's available. Calm-water areas behind large logs in water over 3 feet deep are also very good places to look for big spawners.

Of course, any of these sites must have the proper bottom substrate. If the water clarity is at least fair, you should be able to see the lighter-colored, circular beds. A very large bed (say 3 feet in diameter) wasn't necessarily made by a lunker, but often it indicates that bass at that nesting site are above average in size. A word of caution: don't try to get a look at the fish before you cast to it. More often than not, the fish will be spooked. Spawning fish must be approached with plenty of caution.

Best Times for Big Smallmouth

Lunkers can be taken during the entire fishing season, but three periods are particularly good. The spawn period is one. It lasts only a short time, but many big fish can be taken if you hit a particular waterway during the peak of the spawn and target the best spawning sites. Unfortunately, some state's smallmouth seasons don't open until after the spawn is over. The sentiment behind these closed spring seasons is good, but often it simply means the big fish are killed later in the year. Year-round protection through regulations that mandate the release of large fish is what is really needed to protect and improve our big-bass fisheries.

The second productive period for lunker hunting is the summer; in early through midsummer, all sizes of bass are active. Summer big bass can certainly be taken all day long, but evening is the most consistent time of day. Concentrate on a specific big-bass area during the last hour of daylight. Deliberately plan your outing so you will be fishing over big fish during that last hour. I look forward with anticipation to this magic hour; being on the stream after everyone else has gone home and the big smallies have become more active is a perfect way to end a day of fishing.

The best time of year to catch a trophy smallie is fall. Starting in September in some colder regions and lasting till December in warmer areas, in fall a relatively high number of large fish are taken by those few who seriously fish during this period. This is the time of year bass are at their heaviest, so even a 3½-pound summer fish will weigh at least a few more ounces. Some fall bass really put on the pounds. Several years ago, I caught an October bass that was barely 19 inches long but weighed over 4 pounds. In a span of only a couple of months this fish went from a good river bass to a lunker. The metabolism of fall smallmouth is slowing down, but with appropriate fall techniques fish can be readily taken until water temperatures fall to the mid to upper 40s. Midafternoon (when water temperatures are highest) is the best time of the day to catch fall bass.

TECHNIQUES AND LURES FOR BIG BASS

The question of tackle and techniques is the last piece of the puzzle on catching the biggest smallies. This section will focus on the best techniques for each of the three periods – spawn, summer, and fall.

Big fish on or near their spawning beds can be taken with various slow moving baits. Unweighted pork eels pulled s-l-o-w-l-y over the bed will often elicit a take, as will various slow-sinking, soft plastic baits. Slow-moving topwaters are another favorite of mine during this time. Make sure your casting position allows you to keep the lure over the bed for at least fifteen seconds. If the fish doesn't take after two or three good casts, let the area rest for at least twenty minutes and then try again.

During the midday hours of summer, it's best to concentrate your efforts around (or in) the cover in a big-bass pool. Even if the fish aren't actively feeding, thoroughly working the resting areas can still pay off. Making a dozen or more good casts to a specific spot will increase your chances that one cast comes so close or is so tempting to the inactive fish that she won't be able to resist it.

Fishing underwater boulders is fairly easy. The standard with-the-current retrieve from downstream of the target is normally the best method. Deep-running, high-vibration crankbaits, jigs heavy enough to reach bottom, even properly weighted in-line spinners will all catch behind-the-boulder bass. You can use baits a little larger than those used for smaller fish. All the lures must be able to get down to the bottom where the fish are. Smaller bass will often come up and chase a shallow-running lure, but rarely will the big mamas expend that kind of energy.

Catching lunkers from around wood is a little trickier. Baits that seldom hang up are essential. Standard-weight jigs equipped with weed guards are often good, if you can fish them slowly enough. If the water is extra clear or the fish seem particularly slow, small jigs will sometimes tempt even the biggest bass. A small, lightweight jig slowing settling to the bottom is hard for even a fussy fish to resist. Slow-moving banana-shaped plugs (like big Lazy Ikes or Flatfish) can also be effective for summer "hogs." If you think a particular holding area has a big fish, repeatedly working one of these types of plugs through the spot can pay off.

During summer evenings, big fish often move out of their daytime haunts. Head-of-pool areas near deep-water holding areas shouldn't be overlooked. If the fish have moved up into the shallows they are almost certainly feeding and are probably easier to catch. Large thin minnows, over 4 inches long, and large streamer flies work well under these conditions. If the shallower feeding areas adjacent to deep-water cover spots don't pay off in the evening, don't hesitate to try the deep water.

A favorite technique of mine is to work around logs with a topwater during summer evenings. During midday, the big ones probably won't give a topwater a second glance, but come evening they often nail them with gusto. Various topwaters work at this time, including fly-rod poppers. Try several casts to the same spot before moving on. Just be prepared to set the hook instantly, especially if the strike causes little surface disturbance. Often a light surface strike is a big smallmouth quietly inhaling the lure. What is much harder to be prepared for is the sight of a hog smallie exploding out of the water the second after you set the hook into what you thought was a little fish!

For the most big bass caught per hour of fishing, fall is as productive as the much shorter spawn period. It can also be a very frustrating time unless you fully understand that fall fishing is quite different from summer angling. If you plan to seriously pursue big bronzebacks during the fall cool-water period, make sure you thoroughly read the section on the fall period in the "Different Seasons" chapter.

One particularly effective technique for big fall fish comes to mind: slow and deep fishing with a minnow-tipped jig. The minnow should be several inches long and the undressed lead head can be a bright color like red or white. Of course, other types of slow-moving jigs also produce, but the minnow-tipped ones really shine, especially in the late fall. Slow moving in-line spinners retrieved *steadily,* right along the bottom, can also be very effective if the water clarity is only fair.

"KEEPING" YOUR TROPHY

You may have heard that if a big smallie is taken out of a good spot another will quickly take its place. This is more wishful thinking than actual reality, since the truly large fish are so few in number. However, there *is* one way anyone can catch lunker after lunker from the same place. If you kill it, the chances of catching another any time soon are poor. But if you release it, your chances of catching it again are very high, since you know right where it is and what it likes.

But suppose you get a 4-pound 4-ouncer—the biggest bass you ever caught? "How can I let that go?" you're thinking. Well, I'll tell you how you can both release the trophy to fight again *and* keep it. First, make sure you always carry a camera, a good scale, and a tape. Quickly admire your prize, take its photo, measure its length and girth, and then send it back to its home. Then, when you get back home send the photo and measurements to one of the new fish-mounting enterprises that specialize in graphite mounts. They are absolutely beautiful and amazingly lifelike, they last forever, and the fish on the wall will be an exact replica of the one caught. This way you can indeed have your trophy and release it, too.

12 ⁓⁓

Finesse Fishing:
Catching Extra-Tough Bass

WEBSTER'S DICTIONARY describes *finesse* as "skill, cunning, adroitness." Finesse fishing means all this and more. It means using delicate, subtle, and nonthreatening presentations that make the lure seem extra easy to capture. Finesse fishing often requires extra-slow retrieves, small baits, and light lines. These techniques are employed to catch very inactive fish or heavily fished (smart) bass. Inactive smallmouth have become extremely lethargic because of cold fronts or other reasons. The methods can also apply to cold-water bass and very well fed fish. "Smart" or extremely wary small-mouth develop from both angling pressure and from water types and habitat. A simple rule of thumb is, the clearer and shallower the water, the quicker the fish become hook shy from angling pressure. For them, highly obtrusive baits are seldom productive. Bright, flashing lures, high-vibration crankbaits, or loud-splashing top-waters only turn them off.

When would you need to think about finesse fishing? Let's say its been normal midsummer weather for the past two weeks and the smallies have been striking well. A strong cold front sweeps through and suddenly the fishing seems to shut down. (River bass aren't always turned off by cold fronts, but occasionally they are adversely affected.) Or suppose you head out to a favorite stream, not realizing the watershed has received no rain for almost a month. The river is now a creek, flowing extremely low and clear.

Employing sneak tactics will help you catch extra-spooky clear-water smallies.

A quick check of a few of your favorite stream pools turns up zilch. Or say some Sunday you decide to try a popular river you have heard about. You arrive at this waterway only to discover it runs awfully clear and it's full of anglers. Worse, you discover from conversations with some other fishers that the stream receives a continuous pounding most of the season and the catch rate is extremely low. What to do? Give up fishing and see if your Uncle Joe wants to play pinochle? Not if you're a dedicated smallmouth fan! These are the times to employ some finesse fishing.

FINESSE TECHNIQUES

The one thing that defines finesse fishing is ease of capture, making your presentation too good to resist. This means keeping the presentation in close proximity to the fish (less than 2 feet away) for as long as possible. That means slow retrieves. It can also mean repeated casts to the same place, so that one passes by the fish "just right." Small lures are particularly good for very inactive fish, especially if they seem more irresistible than the natural food present.

Extra-slow retrieves, erratic retrieves, unusual colors, and plenty of undulation all cause your presentation to stand out and tempt inactive fish.

Since you want your baits to pass so close and so slowly by the fish, it's essential to carefully concentrate your casts to very specific spots. River bass that have become very inactive generally move into cover—logs and brush, undercut banks, or deep water. In the pools of some streams, the best cover may be a small depression only slightly deeper than the rest of the pool. This depression may be only a few square feet but still hold several nice fish. Wood cover is also a favorite place for inactive fish; so is aquatic vegetation if it's in water at least 3 feet deep.

FINESSE TACKLE AND LURES AND HOW TO USE THEM

For anglers who already use a long, light-action rod and carry a spool of 4-pound line, adjusting to finesse fishing shouldn't be difficult. If you're accustomed to heavier gear, gearing down to light lures, lines, and rods can take some getting used to. Finesse fishing does require quite light tackle. For spin fishing, 4-pound line is often required to throw lightweight finesse lures. In some cases you can get away with 6-pound test but the lighter line usually works better. Not only do small-diameter lines allow better casting of light baits, but light lines also cut through the water better, allowing you to fish more slowly and deeper with less. Especially in current, where heavy lines are easily swept away, extra-light lines slice through the water with much less pull on them. A flexible rod appropriate for light lines and lures is also needed. The long rod (6½ feet or more) becomes indispensable here; with the extra length, even a whippy rod allows you to set the hook.

Jigs and Jig Techniques

The biggest group of finesse lures is the trusty lead-head jig category. Some particularly good finesse jigs are the small plastic "tube" jigs, small plastic "grubs," extra-small (1/32 ounce) marabou jigs, and the new "weight in the middle" jigs. This last type has its lead in the middle of the hook, which causes the jig to settle more slowly to the bottom; Slo Poke is one brand.

With all these lures, watch your line as the lure slowly falls, both after the initial cast and *each* time you pause in the retrieve. With this technique, sometimes called "fishing the line," you will detect many more strikes than if you only wait to feel the strike. To detect these almost imperceptible takes you need a sharp eye for the little things – little twitches in the line, a little extra slackness, a little pause in line movement. Master the technique and you will be rewarded with many more hooked fish.

All light finesse jigs can be fished in several ways. One method is what I call the "drop" technique. Bring the lure right above the suspected fish-holding spot and allow it to fall slowly near the fish. Use this in areas where the current is slight, and strikes will come while the jig is descending. A variation is the "swim and drop" technique, where the current is a factor. The lure is cast *upstream* of the target and pulled quickly across the surface to the position where it will fall (at an angle) into the fish's strike zone. Remember, a light jig can travel several feet with the current as it settles to the bottom in 5 feet of water. This method takes particular skill in strike detection since plenty of slack line will be present.

A third method is the "drag" technique, where you actually retrieve the lure. Slowly drag the lure along the bottom with occasional slight pauses. Extra-soft plastic-bodied jigs with their heads covered with plastic are particularly good for this; so are small pork Little Crawdads and small Ugly Bugs tipped with a small piece of crawler. This type of lure should look (and feel) so natural that the fish will actually pick it up off the bottom. Of course, set the hook quickly before the bass realizes your offering is a fraud.

Worm and Pork Baits

Another category of finesse lures is unweighted worm and pork baits. Attached to nothing more than a heavy hook, pork eels, pork crawdads, and short, soft plastic worms (ones with lots of tail action) can be swum s-l-o-w-l-y past the fish in areas where the current and the depth aren't great. These baits are especially good for heavily fished smallmouth. Even if the fish instantly recognize every conventional plug, spinner, and jig thrown into the water, these baits are often different enough to fool them. Water-soluble scents applied to these lures sometimes improve their effectiveness. The lures retain scent well and are moving so slowly that fish have enough time to actually smell them.

An uncommon way to fish small (4-inch) plastic worms is the "splitshot" method. Sometimes used by California tournament anglers, this finesse method is seldom used by river fishers, but it can be very effective on clear-water bass. The short worms or leech-style grubs must be made from extra-soft plastic. If you can't find them in the tackle shop, pour your own and make super-soft, lifelike baits. Rig the worm Texas style, with the hook point embedded in the lure. Use a hook made of fine wire and super-sharp, so the worm will be very lightweight and you can set the hook with light line. Clamp just enough splitshot 16 inches above the lure so it will get to the bottom. Slowly drag the splitshot over the bottom with a reel-and-pause technique, while the lure darts just off the bottom.

Miniature Baits

The last category of finesse spinning lures is miniature versions of regular smallmouth baits. Tiny plugs like ultrasmall Rebel thin minnows and tiny Flatfish are very good. Very small in-line spinners also produce on occasion. All these lures must have good action at very slow retrieves. They should all be worked slowly and close to the bottom, and they're especially productive when you repeatedly retrieve them through the same area.

Since so many finesse lures are small and lightweight, an easy way to increase your casting distance with them should be of interest. Actually I use this casting technique for all my light spinning and didn't realize until a few years ago that many anglers never use this style. Instead of winding the lure almost to the rod tip and flicking the rod backward so that the lure bends the rod, do a "pendulum cast" – let the lure dangle about 2 feet below the rod tip, then tip the rod backward so the lure swings pendulum style. This puts added bend into the rod as the cast goes forward. It somewhat resembles a fly rodder's roll cast. With the technique, even lures

Miniature plugs on light line were productive on this extra-clear Mid-South stream.
Lyn Verthein.

under $1/16$ ounce can be cast quite accurately up to 60 feet. Of course, you need a limber rod and light line for this pendulum cast.

FINESSE FLY FISHING

When it comes to finesse fishing, the fly rodder is more fortunate than the spin fisher. Fishing small and lightweight baits is a breeze on the long rod compared to the trouble it is with spinning tackle. Deciding when and where to use finesse fishing is the same no matter what type of equipment you use. And with-the-current retrieves are the most effective with fly tackle just as with spin gear. For streams without great depth (6 feet or under), the same tackle used in everyday fly angling, including floating lines, will do fine for finesse fishing. Perhaps the only tackle modification would be slightly longer leaders of 9 or 10 feet with tippets no heavier than 4-pound test. In areas with deeper water, a switch to a Sink-Tip or even a full sinking line may be in order. Getting the fly down near the bottom and keeping it there are essential, and if the depth and current require sinking lines, you should oblige.

Detecting strikes may be a challenge. The light "takes" of sluggish deep-water fish require plenty of attentiveness. Besides learning to recognize how light strikes feel, you should watch the line or the leader for anything out of the ordinary. And if you are using a floating line, put two strike indicators on the leader, one near the leader-line joint and the other about 3 feet farther down the leader.

As for what flies to use, many standard smallmouth patterns work fine. Often the flies should be in smaller sizes and weighted just enough to get them to the bottom. Heavily weighted flies settle to the bottom too quickly and must be retrieved more quickly than slow-sinking varieties. Smaller "trout-sized" Woolly Buggers in dark colors, but tied on a short-shank number 4 or 6 hook, are very good. Simple crawfish patterns (with a chenille body) in a smaller size are another good choice. Sculpin and leech patterns are also effective in getting inactive fish to strike. All these flies should be fished slow and deep.

A somewhat different enticement is the previously mentioned spinner-fly combination. The spinner blade can and should be very small and must rotate at slow speed. This is the lure to use when you are trying to make the fish strike by repeatedly casting to the same spot. It can also be fished a little faster than regular flies, so you can cover the water a little quicker.

The next time you've tried all the conventional lures and techniques and you still can't cure the fish of their case of lockjaw, try the finesse method. It takes some time and skill to perfect, but the satisfaction of producing fish when everything (and everyone) else fails is worth it.

13 ～～

Special Tips
for Those Just Starting Out

THIS CHAPTER IS FOR EVERYONE who is new to stream small-mouth angling. Some of the tips have been mentioned in other parts of the book and are presented again as a condensation. Other advice here is new. All together, these ideas can make your progression into stream smallmouth fishing quicker, easier, and more enjoyable.

STARTING TACKLE AND
STREAM SKILLS

As you have gathered by now, I don't believe in expensive tackle as the sole key to angling happiness, and this is especially true for those just starting out. It doesn't make sense to run out and spend $500 on equipment before you know if you're going to like the sport. At the same time, being adequately equipped is important even for the newcomer. So beg, borrow, or buy a decent outfit. If you're a spin fisher and have never used a rod longer than 5½ feet, start with a 6½-foot rod instead of a 7-footer; it will cost less and take less getting used to. If you aren't used to hooking and handling strong fish on light-action rods, get a rod rated light-medium instead of light. Factory rods of this type are relatively common and low cost. Or perhaps you could borrow one for a few trips. The idea is to start out with a rod a little heavier and a little shorter than what you may want after a season or two. The same for lines; if you're not used to handling strong fish on 4- and 6-pound line, stick with 8-pound test for a while.

Advice for the fly fisher follows this same logic. If you are inexperienced with handling strong fish on light tackle don't head out to the bass stream with a 4- or 5-weight trout and bluegill rod. A 7-weight would be more appropriate, at least until you get more experience. The same with leaders; 8-pound tippets will do fine for most smallmouth angling and give you much less grief than lighter leaders.

Lures

Many skilled anglers know that lightweight jigs and unweighted in-line spinners are often deadly, but these types of lures can be frustrating to the inexperienced. A beginning stream angler needs lures that are easy to use but still do a good job on the fish. Weighted in-line spinners, shallow-running thin minnows, and shallow-running crankbaits are all good choices. Stick with ⅛-ounce or heavier baits for the first several outings before trying lighter stuff. Just make sure all the hooks on your lures are very sharp. Far too many anglers, especially the less experienced, pay no attention to their hooks and never sharpen them. If you are used to nonjumping or soft-mouthed fish like trout or walleye you'll be surprised at how much harder smallies are to hook and hold. Buy a hook hone and learn how to use it.

Casting

Another thing you can do to improve your stream-fishing success is be conscious of your casting. If your previous angling didn't require accurate casting, there are a couple things you can do to make your bass fishing more enjoyable. First, stay away from waters that re-quire precision casting: narrow streams with heavily wooded banks or lots of logs, or very shallow water with lots of rocks. The second is – practice! Don't be afraid to go out and throw a lure around in the yard or in a park. Practice throwing a ⅛-ounce lure (take the hooks off first) under low-hanging branches. See if you can hit a 1-yard target from 20 to 75 feet. And while you're actually out fishing, be conscious of how your casting is coming along. Don't expect to make perfect casts every time, but try to gradually improve over the season.

In general, take it easy as you're getting started. Don't overdo it during your first trips. Too many people new to stream fishing try to set endurance records during their first outings. A few hours of hard fishing is plenty for one day. If you really want to go out for the entire day, don't try to pound the water nonstop for twelve hours. Schedule three or four rest stops and a long lunch break. If you're floating, make sure the water miles are short. Rivers are wonderful places to spend your day, but if you want to fish while you're there, you'll do better with 5 miles of river than 15. And of course, try to pick good weather and good water conditions. If it's a cold spring day and the water is still cold and discolored, wait until conditions are more favorable. If it's midsummer and it rains 4 inches the day before you plan to hit the stream, don't just go

This angler hooked a good one after parking the canoe and fishing a likely spot on foot.

anyway and hope for the best. Chances are, fishing will be awful under those conditions for even the best anglers. Having several disappointing trips while you are just getting into the sport is not the way to start any activity.

A Checklist of Items Needed

It's an excellent idea to draw up a checklist of items needed for the sport and those you already possess. That includes not only visible objects like rods and lures, but also a number of other less tangible things. First, consider what specific type of stream angling you are interested in. Canoe floating? Wade only? Then, what does that type of fishing require? What kind of watercraft is necessary? What physical condition do you need to wade fish in your area? Third, how do you measure up? Have you ever done any wade fishing? Can you handle a canoe or johnboat in moving water?

Take a few minutes to jot down all the relevant points you can think of. Be as honest as you can about your present status – not just what tackle you already possess but also other things like previous river experience and your physical condition. (If you're really out of shape, you should plan a realistic step-by-step program.) Actually jotting things down on paper should let you see exactly what you need to get started, and should reassure you that you're not forgetting something important.

FISHING WITH AN EXPERIENCED ANGLER OR GUIDE

Actually spending some time on the water with a professional guide or a highly experienced angler is a very good way for those just starting out to quickly develop their skills. It's also wise to fish with a guide or knowledgeable angler when trying a new area or new types of water, or when fishing for big bass.

The number of fishing guides that offer river smallmouth trips is still small, but it's a growing field. Especially in the East, new guide services operating on the larger smallmouth rivers are popping up all the time. Even in the Midwest, more and more guides specialize in river fishing. These trips often combine bass fishing with walleye, pike, and such. If you want the luxury of a guided smallmouth outing (and are willing to pay for it), by all means try one.

Before you book a guide, spend a few minutes thinking about your goals. Do you simply want an easy outing, one where the guide does almost everything? Or do you want a trip focusing on catching *big* smallies? Or maybe a trip where you can learn a lot? These trips are quite different from one another, and not all guide services provide them. If you want to learn a lot, it's important to find a guide who will teach you some things. Not all of them are as articulate as you might like, and some don't want to give away their trade secrets. If you see the trip primarily as a way to learn how to fish, don't try to discover all the guide's hotspots. Guides don't usually want to see their previous clients coming back to the places they showed them the week before. Besides, learning proper techniques is far more valuable than uncovering particular fishing spots.

When you talk to prospective guides, be honest about your interests. Without approaching them in a demanding way, simply state what your interests are and listen to what they say. It's also a good idea to say you are primarily a catch-and-release angler, if you are. Guides may be more willing to show you techniques, knowing you aren't going to be out on the river depleting the bass population the next day. And I strongly recommend that you *not* patronize any guide service that is still heavily into catch and kill. Besides causing serious damage to our fisheries, these guides aren't good ones to learn from, since they're too busy trying to load the boat with fish to talk about how-to's.

You have a right to expect certain things from the guide, but miracles aren't one of them. Don't expect a guarantee of hordes of fish and don't expect to become an instant expert. Don't expect the guide to control the weather or river conditions. But do expect your guide to provide the kind of general experience you agreed on beforehand. Do listen to your guide and follow his or her recommendations on lures and techniques.

Finding a Knowledgeable Fishing Partner

What if you don't have a guide available to fish with, but still want the experience of fishing with a knowledgeable angler? There are lots of anglers out there you can learn from, people who enjoy showing new converts the joys of moving-water angling; it's just a matter of finding them. If you already know a friend or relative who fits this category, you've got it made. Otherwise, joining a fishing organization is one good way of finding knowledgeable and gregarious anglers. Going to fishing seminars and programs also has potential. Even posting your name on a tackle shop bulletin board will often uncover friendly, helpful smallmouth fans. Finding good fishing partners may take creative energy, but if you put a little effort into it you should be successful.

When you find a potential partner, be friendly, polite, flexible, and genuinely appreciative – not demanding. You aren't hiring this person and shouldn't expect him or her to cater to your every need. Offer to drive and provide lunch for both of you. And don't try to pretend you know more than you do. The best policy is to admit you are a novice, but are eager to learn and appreciate the opportunity to fish with the person. The most important thing to look for is an ability to explain things. But even fishing with a "silent Sam" type is better than with no one at all. Stay a discrete distance away and watch closely what your partner does.

These tips should give you a head start as a new stream smallmouth angler. If you are coming to stream fishing from a lake-fishing background, pay particular attention to the chapters on aspects unique to the stream setting, such as the chapters on currents and on-foot fishing. If you are pretty new to angling in general, at first stick with the basics: decent casting, hook setting, and proper wading or boat handling. And no matter how much you know, don't forget there's always more to learn.

14 ~~∽

Bonus Catches: Other Stream Species

SMALLMOUTH RIVERS ARE HOME to many other fish species commonly or occasionally taken by sport fishers. With a quick mental tally, I can recall over two dozen species I catch (at least occasionally) while smallmouth fishing, ranging from the "glamorous" muskie and brown trout all the way to the "lowly" creek chub or fallfish. I really appreciate this rich diversity in the waters I fish because, as much as I enjoy catching bronzebacks, I also enjoy the challenge and change of pace of other species.

Just about all anglers have their preferred fish species, but I can't understand the loathing some seem to have for other fish. Though I'm a devoted smallmouth angler, I think hooking a fast, powerful channel catfish is very exciting. Even hitting a pod of feisty sunfish puts a smile on my face. To me, a "sport fish" is any kind I can catch on artificials and that gives a respectable tussle. So what if the freshwater drum (sheephead) isn't highly regarded in many angling circles? This and other unappreciated species will nail your lures with gusto and provide fine sport on light tackle, adding to the quality of your stream fishing.

We don't have room to deal thoroughly with the great variety of fish species that our smallmouth rivers hold. Instead, I've included eight categories of fish encompassing twenty species – the most widespread fish and the ones most likely to be caught by moving-water anglers. This guide will give some basic information on geographical distribution and types of streams frequented for each species, but it will be up to you to find out exactly what fish are available locally.

The eastern mountains are a major dividing line separating the extensive Mississippi drainage system from the Atlantic drainages. Historically, this meant a number of river species native to the Mississippi drainage were absent from Atlantic drainage waters, and vice versa. Some of this natural separation has been overcome by humans planting various species into new waters. (For instance, the smallmouth was first introduced into Atlantic drainages in the nineteenth century.) So looking at the original species range maps is of only limited value. Studying recent and thorough fisheries surveys of individual rivers is the best way to determine if a particular fish is present.

A little educated investigation (knowing where to look and what to look for) can save you months of "blind" on-the-water investigation. Use some of the basic methods described in Chapter 2 to find what other bonus fish are present in your streams. Overall, this chapter is oriented toward helping anglers increase their fishing enjoyment by learning how to catch some of these other species along with the smallmouth.

Smallmouth fan Kurt Sleighter enjoys including a nice-sized drum in his day's catch.

Bonus Stream Species

Species	Attributes	Regions
Pickerel	Common in many streams, strikes well	East, parts of Mid-South and Canada
Pike	Large size, good fighter, strikes well	Midwest, western Canada
Muskie	Very large size, hard fighter	Certain streams: Midwest, Mid-South, East
Walleye or Sauger	Challenging catch, good tasting	Midwest, parts of Mid-South and Canada
Channel Catfish	Good size, hard fighter	Mid-South, Midwest
Panfish	Very common, easy to catch	All regions have some species
Trout	Challenging catch	Occasional: East, Midwest, Canada, Western U.S.
Largemouth	Fair size, strikes well	Mid-South, occasional elsewhere
Spotted Bass	Hard fighter, strikes well	Mid-South
Fallfish or Chub	Very common, easy to catch	Fallfish: East, parts of Mid-South. Chub: Midwest
Drum	Good size, strikes well	Midwest, parts of Mid-South
Mooneye	Plentiful in certain streams, can be taken on dry flies	Midwest
White Bass	Hard fighter, large schools	Mid-South, parts of Midwest

THE PIKE FAMILY: CHAIN PICKEREL, MUSKIE, AND PIKE

I like catching these fish. Not just the mighty muskie or big pike but even the smaller pickerel quickens my pulse. They vary greatly in size, but all have some common characteristics. All are long and sleek and built for bursts of high speed. All feed predominantly on other fish, using their large mouths and sharp teeth to seize even quite large prey. They prefer cover in slack-water areas, rocketing out when potential prey ventures too close. Rocky substrates aren't needed; sand or even mud bottoms will do just fine, so long as the current isn't too strong and some cover is nearby, especially vegetation or wood.

Pickerel

The chain pickerel (not to be confused with the much smaller grass or redfin pickerels) is largely a fish of Atlantic drainages. An adaptable fish, it does well from the warm creeks of south Florida to the very cool waters of New England. Unfortunately for the eastern angler, this "little pike" doesn't approach the size of its much larger cousins. In most rivers, a 2½-pound chain pickerel is a large fish. The pickerel loves aquatic vegetation. If it isn't available, wood cover or even large rocks will be used as holding areas in slow-water areas. Pickerel, like pike, are active in cold water and can be caught year around. In the South, open-water pickerel fishing in the winter months is a definite possibility. These fish can be caught on a wide variety of baits, including most of the standard smallmouth lures. Medium-sized thin minnows and bright spinners are some of the best. When the pickerel are finicky, less common pickerel baits like plastic worms or pork eels will tempt many fish into striking.

Muskie

The muskie or muskellunge, of several strains, is native to or has been introduced to numerous rivers around the Great Lakes and south into West Virginia, Kentucky, and Tennessee. Most people think of muskie as only a big-river fish, but fair numbers of intermediate-sized rivers also hold them, for example the Flambeau River in Wisconsin, the Juniata in Pennsylvania, and the Mud River in West Virginia. Occasionally even much smaller waterways produce muskies – usually not big fish or a lot of them, but if the stream is a tributary of a larger, quality muskie river it pays to check these small waters out. Recently, I caught two 7-pound muskies (on two consecutive casts!) from a pool only 35 feet wide in a small Wisconsin creek. Even a 5-pound muskie on light tackle is a tremendous catch. Float-sized rivers can see considerably larger specimens – 12- to 20-pounders as infrequent trophies, 5- to 8-pound fish as everyday catches.

Few waters support high numbers of muskies of any size, which is one reason this fish is held in such high regard by many fishers. This comparative rarity will also lead to high frustration if you go out expecting lots of action. Concentrate on bass or other species and count your blessings if you occasionally catch a muskie. Of course, learning a few things about this uncommon fish and how to fish for it will make the blessing-counting more frequent.

Most of the better-sized muskie will be found in the largest pools in a river. The larger the fish, the more room it needs. Some good cover in that pool is also required. Downed trees, root systems, boulders, and weed patches all qualify as acceptable cover, provided they are in slow water at least several feet deep. Unless the muskie population is unusually high, there may be only one good area in a mile or more of water. For a 7-mile float this could mean only five to six areas would warrant muskie fishing.

Conventional muskie tackle is vastly different from smallmouth tackle. The incredibly stiff rods, heavy lines, and big baits used by many hard-core muskie fans aren't needed for part-time river muskie fishing. If you are bringing along an extra outfit, a long rod that will handle baits up to ¾ ounce and 12- or 14-pound line will do as long as the river-weed growth isn't heavy. Medium-sized in-line spinners with big bucktail dressings and large thin minnows are good river lures. If weed growth is very high, weedless spoons with pork frogs are hard to beat. In many areas, purple, black, and white are the most popular colors for muskie spinners and spoons. Various types of noisy topwaters also take their share of fish, including large fly-rod poppers.

Summer evenings are good times to use noisy surface lures. During the summer months in general, a relatively fast retrieve often produces the most strikes or follows. (Muskies are notorious for following and not striking.) However, in the spring considerably slower retrieves and smaller baits often take large fish.

River muskie can really turn on during August, especially in Michigan, Wisconsin, and Minnesota. This is the best time for the novice muskie angler. Keep a separate outfit rigged up for muskie and thoroughly work the best-looking spots when you float into them. If no fish are raised after twenty or thirty minutes of hard fishing, move on to the next area. Hitting several likely areas in a day gives you a good chance of raising at least a fish or two. Fall, while not as consistent for high numbers of fish as the late summer period, often produces the biggest fish of the year.

Pike

The pike is common in many rivers in the central and northern regions of the Mississippi drainage. Far more numerous than the muskellunge, the pike grows to large sizes (over 15 pounds in some streams) and strikes and fights well. Many American anglers insist upon calling pike "northern" pike, but since there are no "southern" or "western" pike, I'm sticking with just "pike."

Access to flooded vegetation, usually flooded marshes, during early spring spawning determines whether a river has a naturally reproducing pike population. In the better parts of the pike's range, like Ontario and the Upper Great Lakes states, even quite small creeks will have some of these river rockets. In more southerly climes, like Indiana and Ohio, pike seem to be more restricted to larger waters. In any part of its range, the best pike rivers are rarely the area's best smallmouth waters. The pike prefers slow water with plenty of wood or weed cover, not the rocky riffles of good smallie water, but a great many streams have both species. Sadly, the pike in the relatively fast-flowing and rocky streams are seldom heavyweights. Some people have difficulty unhooking pike. If you plan to catch pike, make sure you carry needle-nose pliers and a jaw spreader. This will permit much easier hook removal and also keep you from injuring the fish during a difficult hook removal. Bending the barbs down on your lures also makes hook removal much easier.

The best way to fish for pike while on a smallmouth trip is

to have two outfits along (if you're floating). A 6½-foot, medium-action spinning rod loaded with 10-pound test will handle most river pike. A comparable-weight bait-casting outfit, while not necessary, will also do. Larger in-line spinners with big dressings and various largemouth-size safety-pin spinners are consistent producers. The number 4 Mepps spinner with a large white or orange bucktail has caught hundreds of river pike for me. Moderate-speed retrieves for pike are generally best; the fast retrieves so popular for muskies seldom produce many pike. A bait seldom used for pike, but a very good one, is the jig—not any old jig, but one with a large body and tail. When pike are in an inactive mood, a large and tantalizing jig hopped along the bottom produces strikes when little else will. I like a ¼-ounce jig head with a large plastic double-tail body in yellow or white.

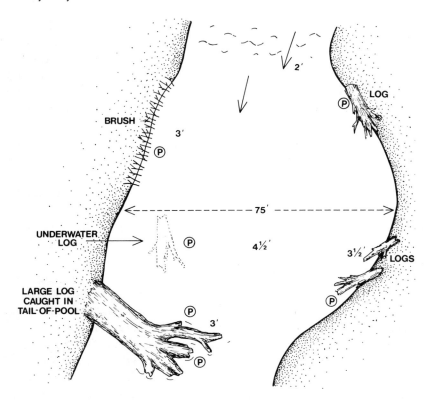

Pike and pickerel spots. Since most of the wood cover is in 3 or more feet of water, most of the fish in the pool relate to the wood. "P" designates pickerel or pike.

If pike exist in good numbers in a river, fly fishing can be very good. Good-sized flashy streamers work very well, if used on a 7-weight rod. With most spinners and all flies and jigs, a good bite-proof leader is mandatory. Thirty-pound monofilament will prevent most (not all) biteoffs, but the best is a very flexible and small-diameter steel leader. Don't use one of those very large diameter, stiff leaders commonly sold as pike leaders; they impair a lure's action and scare off many fish, especially bass.

Pike can be caught from early spring to freezeup. Lots of small fish can be caught in spring, but midsummer is actually better for larger pike *if* some cooler water can be found. Small pike will stay in very warm water and continue to feed, but big fish over 7 or 8 pounds quit feeding and are adversely affected by warm water (over 70 degrees) so they seek out cool water. If even a small pocket of cool water can be found during hot summer conditions, some very good fish can be taken. Mouths of cold trout streams and cold spring seepages are good places to find big summer pike. The easiest time to catch good pike is in the fall when the water has fallen into the 50s. The fish are actively feeding, heavy weed growth if present in the summer is now gone, and big fish strike very well. In just the last few years, I've caught several pike over 11 pounds during this fast fall period—from streams almost too small to float.

Pike over 5 pounds, if taken on light tackle, are very exciting catches—and increasingly rare. These fine fish are far too valuable to be killed. If you really want a pike or two to eat, kill a couple of 2-pounders and release the larger fish so you and others can catch them again and again.

WALLEYE AND SAUGER

Everybody and his uncle knows about the walleye or sauger fishing below dams on big rivers. Just try to find a little elbow room below Mississippi or Ohio River dams in the spring! But few of these same anglers realize the walleye also inhabits many other much smaller rivers. In the upper Midwest (Michigan, Wisconsin, and Minnesota) and Ontario, even many small creeks have good year-round populations. Farther south (Illinois, Indiana, and Missouri) and east (Pennsylvania), walleye, while not common in creeks, are still present in slightly larger waters. So if walleye or sauger are native or have been widely introduced to your region, don't automatically assume they're only in the big rivers. (For those who don't know, the sauger, sometimes called sand pike, is similar to the walleye, sort of a smaller cousin with a blotchy color pattern. Because of their similar habits, I'll talk about these two together.)

The walleye and sauger are not exactly hard fighters, but their legendary table qualities and reputation for finickiness make them a tempting challenge. Also, stream walleye fishing has some advantages over lake fishing. River walleye can only go about 6 or 7 feet deep, and they are not as susceptible to cold fronts as their lake-dwelling cousins. And unless the water clarity is exceptionally high, river fish are not nearly as light sensitive. This all means that you can catch stream walleye in relatively shallow water, during cold fronts, and during midday.

Finding Stream Walleye

During the daylight hours, walleye will normally be found near the bottom in several possible holding areas. The easiest places to fish, and the most popular, are below dams and falls. If these exist on a river that has walleye, some fish can be found below them at all times of the year. Unfortunately, fishing below dams during weekends is often a crowded affair; if possible, try weekdays. On smaller streams, the deepest pools hold most daytime walleye. If you learn to recognize them, you can focus on walleye in these relatively few producing pools and concentrate on smallmouth or other species in between. In larger waters, the *lower* end, or tail, of the pool is the place to try. Active daytime fish can also be found in deep runs (glides) and at the merger of two channels, if they are at least 4 feet deep. Even in midsummer, fish can be taken from all these places. These holding or feeding spots don't have to have rock bottom; gravel or sandy substrates also attract walleye or sauger. Evenings or cloudy days make for a little better fishing, but even during sunny conditions a thorough angler can still take some walleye. The secret is getting something right down in front of the fish.

How to Catch Walleye and Sauger

Day in and day out, the jig is still the best all-around lure for walleye. Plastic, marabou, and pork-dressed jigs all produce. They

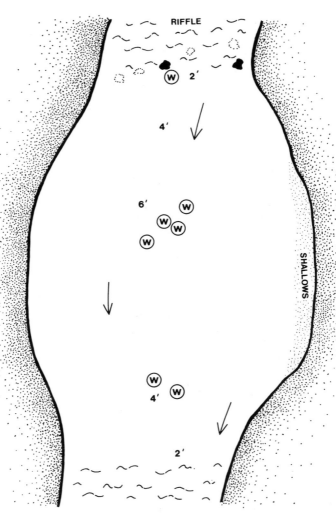

A walleye or sauger pool. The fish at the tail of the pool will be the most active. On shallower streams, look for resting walleye in the deepest pool in a river section. "W" designates walleye or sauger.

must be slowly worked right along the bottom. The jig weight must be heavy enough to get to the bottom in the current, but light enough that it *slowly* settles down after each rise. Yellow is my most consistent color, with white and chartreuse right behind.

The walleye strike is often nothing more than a very light tap, so pay very close attention. If you do receive a strike or tap, work that same area carefully. Often three or four fish can be taken from an area of just a few square feet if you repeatedly work your lure through it.

Another way to catch summer walleye is to work a crankbait along the bottom of a holding area. High-vibration "cranks" catch some very good river walleye, and the strike is much easier to detect. In the summer, activity increases in late evening and sometimes the fish move toward the surface or shallow areas. During this magic half hour of twilight, you can often take walleye near the surface on shallow-running thin minnow plugs and such.

Spring, when many river fishers traditionally try for walleye, can be a good time, but often the water is high and discolored. You'll need heavier and more visible jigs; fluorescent orange or chartreuse are good spring colors. You may also need to bundle up to ward off the cold or rain.

But don't limit yourself to just spring or summer fishing. Fall is probably the best time to consistently catch walleye. Even when late-season water temperatures are in the low 40s and the smallie is almost comatose, walleye will actively feed. Sure, their strikes will be extra light, but if your offering is presented slow and deep enough they will take it. Look for fall fish in the same places they were in summer, and when you find them invariably several fish will be in the same spot. If you have great difficulty in detecting strikes or hooking fish, tipping a plain lead head with a minnow may help. This "natural" jig often causes the fish to hold on a little longer after striking, and occasionally the actual numbers of strikes will be higher.

CHANNEL CATFISH

Here's a great fighting bonus catch. Hook a 3-pound river channel catfish on a smallmouth outfit, and be prepared for incredibly fast and powerful runs. Hook a 6-pounder, and go home wondering

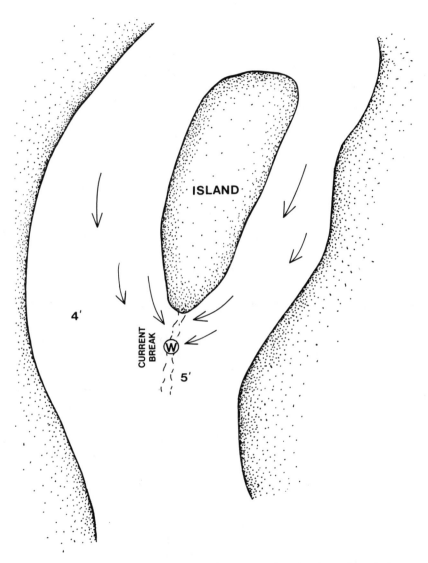

The current break created by the merging of two channels is best for walleye if it's over 4 feet deep.

what the heck broke your line. A lot of people use "stink baits" or other such concoctions, but the channel catfish also feeds heavily on live minnows and crawfish and strikes artificials that look like them. I catch fair numbers of cats every year on jigs, crankbaits, in-line spinners, even deep-running flies.

The channel catfish is widely distributed in the eastern half of the United States and southern Canada (even Manitoba has some huge ones). Don't confuse the channel cat with other catfish or bull-heads, since other related species are different in habits. Although channel catfish do best in large and intermediate waterways, some smaller tributaries hold good numbers. As their name implies, channel catfish do fine in rivers with substantial current flows; in some rivers, especially below dams where food is abundant, they can be found in very strong currents. At the same time, they do fine in rivers with almost no current. In other words, a catfish river can be just about any stream except cold and tiny trout streams. The fish in smaller streams, however, do not attain great size; 2- to 3-pound stream catfish are very respectable and those over 6 pounds are real trophies.

In classic smallmouth waterways (with well-defined rocky riffle–pool structure), catfish are found in many of the same places as the bass. They hold deep in the pools during periods of inactivity and when actively feeding, they move up toward the food-rich riffles just like smallies. In slower rivers with more sand or mud bottom and submerged logs, cats spend a lot of the day holding behind these logs. In this type of river, the fish move upstream to shallow flats or sandbar dropoffs to feed. In all rivers, this movement toward shallower water to feed is often stimulated by low evening light conditions or rising water.

Obviously the easiest time to catch channel cats is when they are actively feeding, and that means evening. The biggest problem with any evening fishing is its limited duration. An hour or two of great fishing is fine, but what about all the other hours in a fishing day? Even though the fish are just sitting around (so to speak) during much of the day, some can still be caught. Bait fishers get them by soaking bait right in front of their noses (literally). Working a scented jig right along the bottom of holding pools or around logs is also good. Water-soluble crawfish scents applied to plastic or pork-bodied jigs are good. A crawfish tail on a brown marabou jig is another good one. Fishing around logs requires snag-guard–equipped jigs and a little heavier line unless you are able to vertical jig from a craft. (See the chapter on float fishing for more on vertical jigging in rivers.) Crawfish-colored crankbaits near the bottom also catch daytime or evening catfish. The fly fisher can take some cats with Woolly Buggers or large nymph patterns, providing they are worked deep.

Areas below dams often have tremendous numbers of catfish, especially where high numbers of dead forage fish come over or through the dam. These are the best places to catch daytime cats on artificials, since the fish are so concentrated. Under these conditions, bright and lighter-colored lures are good. Even extra-flashy stuff like silver-tinsel jigs and silver-bladed in-line spinners with a white ripple rind dressing are productive if the water clarity below the dam is low.

Catfish are very active in high-temperature water and in many areas, the "dog days" of August are doggone good for cats. So even if other species seem to be tough to catch during late summer, Old Whiskers will gladly oblige. And if you want to stay and fish after dark with chicken liver or a commercial catfish bait, the fishing will probably be nothing short of fast and furious. Smaller channel catfish in particular are fine eating. This fish is generally more abundant than more sought-after species like bass, trout, or walleye, so killing a few for supper won't hurt the population much.

PANFISH

"Panfish" is a catch-all term that includes many species of smaller fish. While it has no scientific accuracy, it is commonly used by anglers, so I'll use it too. The most common stream panfish are rock bass, warmouth, crappie, green sunfish, redbreast sunfish, longear sunfish, and a few other less common sunfish species. Almost every smallmouth stream has at least two species in the panfish category, although most of them don't grow very large. However, they're eager to strike and can give good action during periods of smallmouth inactivity. All of them seek out available cover and calm water and congregate in small schools.

Rock Bass

The rock bass is the most widespread stream panfish. Thousands of creeks and rivers from Canada to the southern states have the hard-striking rock bass in them. It is also one of the larger panfish species, with some specimens weighing a pound or more. The biggest rock bass seem to inhabit streams with low smallmouth populations, so don't be surprised if the rock bass in your favorite smallie streams rarely grow over half a pound. However, even small ones will strike surprisingly large baits. I've often caught rock bass the same length as the lure.

Individual rock bass can be found in typical smallmouth areas, but concentrations of them will be around wood cover. If a pool has a tree or big log in it, a number of "rockies" will be tightly schooled around it. Get your lure into this cover and you'll get repeated strikes. Sinking plugs, jigs, spinners, and streamer flies all interest rock bass. The type of lure isn't as important as getting it *very* close to the fish.

Sunfish

Sunfish are another common resident of many streams – the red-breast sunfish in the East, the green sunfish in the Midwest, and the beautiful longear sunfish in the Ozarks. In northern areas sunfish seldom grow over ⅓ pound, but in some Mid-South streams sunfish grow to at least ½ pound. Even small sunfish are very feisty and readily strike small lures. These fish, like the rock bass, are often found around logs and brush, but they prefer vegetation. Slow-flowing streams with lots of aquatic vegetation have the most and biggest sunfish.

Like smallmouth, "sunnies" are nest builders. During spawning (which occurs after smallmouth spawning) the males are absolutely ferocious. Dropping any sort of lure close to their bed elicits an immediate strike. With polarized glasses you can see clusters of their small, light-colored beds. This is a good time to introduce someone to the joys of surface fly fishing. Just make sure to use a small enough popper. At other times of the year poppers also produce, as do very small jigs, spinners, and small weighted flies.

Crappies

Crappies, while not as common in rivers as they are in lakes, do exist in good numbers in some medium and large rivers. Logs and brush in slack-water areas are their favorite haunts, although under-cut banks sometimes hold fish. Like the other panfish, they bunch into small schools if sufficient numbers are present. Look for wood cover in backwaters or side pools.

Catching lots of crappies on artificials can be tough unless you observe two rules. Use *tiny* jigs or small streamer or nymph patterns, and make extra-slow retrieves. Use a tiny jig ($1/32$-ounce rabbit-hair ones are good) below a small bobber, and you can make a very slow retrieve without hanging up on the bottom. If you barely inch the jig along while it's suspended at least 6 inches off the bottom, even the fussiest crappie will strike—or rather, lightly inhale—the jig. Pay very close attention to the small float. If it does anything unusual, *lightly* set the hook; remember the crappie's nick-name, "Paper Mouth."

TROUT

The adaptable brown, the still-popular rainbow, and to a lesser extent the native brookie, have been (re)introduced into many smaller cool-water streams throughout the smallmouth's range. In many states, trout inhabit the cooler, upper end of the creek and smallmouth predominate in the lower end. In a portion of stream the species may overlap. This mixed zone may only be for a mile or two or it may be 20 miles. Streams that have native smallmouth but are heavily stocked with trout also offer good potential for mixed fishing. Some trout-crazy states, like Pennsylvania, annually stock thousands of stream miles. Some of the sections are pretty marginal for trout and are better suited for bass, so catching both species is very likely.

Another place to catch both trout and bass is on smallmouth rivers that have numerous cold-water trout tributaries. Some trout will invariably move downstream to the mouths of the cold tribu-taries. If the larger river has some cold-water spring "holes," trout will also find them and take up residence. Sometimes these cool areas are many miles downstream of "official" trout water. You need a thermometer to check for these cooler spring areas or tributary mouths. In the summer, look for water less than 70 degrees.

Rainbow trout are notorious for leaving the places they were stocked and occasionally turn up far downstream. Larger brown trout will also head downstream looking for bigger waters. So you may not catch lots of fish, but they will probably be above average in size. The first step in finding out whether trout and bass overlap in any streams is to get a listing of all designated trout waters in a region. See if any of these streams are also bass waters farther downstream or if a number of trout creeks flow into a bass river in the same area.

Fly fishers can easily combine trout and bass fishing by simply carrying both larger bass flies and smaller stuff more appropriate for trout. Small streamers and nymphs are always good rainbow or brown producers and will take some smallies besides. But that old reliable, the Woolly Bugger, may be the best fly for catching both trout and bass. Of course, if you see fish rising to a surface hatch, appropriate dry flies are called for.

Spin Fishing for Trout

If you don't fly fish, pack a few special lures and a spool of 4-pound line, and you're ready for trout. For those unfamiliar with spin fishing for trout, it's important to know about a basic color scheme. As a general rule, silver is best for rainbow trout, gold is better for browns, and brookies will often take either color. Small gold-bladed spinners (like Panther Martins or Rooster Tails) really turn on the browns, while these same types in silver excite the rainbows. The same goes for small spoons ($1/8$ to $1/32$ ounce): gold for browns, silver for the rainbows. Small plugs are also excellent trout baits. Tiny thin minnow plugs made by Rebel, in the appropriate belly colors, are my favorite trout tempters.

The nice thing about these small plugs is that smallmouth also think they're great food. All these minnow-imitating lures are particularly good for larger trout, which feed on minnows more than small trout do. If the trout are in limited areas (like creek mouths), just switch to the lighter line and smaller baits at these places. The rest of the time use what's best for smallmouth. If the trout and smallies are mixed throughout the stream, use the lures for the species that predominates and catch the other one as a bonus.

LARGEMOUTH AND SPOTTED BASS

Largemouth

Largemouth bass, though not originally native to many rivers, have been so widely introduced around the continent that a few turn up in almost any stream. The largemouth doesn't do well in good smallmouth habitat, but occupies the cover-laden, slack-water areas. If a river has mixed habitat – both rocky pools and riffles and wood or weeds in slack water – the two bass species can coexist well. Many Mid-South hill streams have a combination of rocky riffle areas and slow deep pools where largemouth and smallmouth co-exist in good numbers, with each occupying its favored niche. On rivers of this type you can concentrate on smallies in the best small-mouth habitat and switch to bigmouths in their areas of concentra-tion. If the river has old connecting channels with cover in them, the largemouth will definitely gravitate there. Otherwise, banks with heavy cover will draw them. Another place to find large-mouth is in smallie streams with lots of small dams on them; the small ponds created by the dams are invariably stocked with large-mouth. Some of these fish will swim upstream into the river itself and can be taken by the smallmouth angler a mile or two above the impoundment. Good baits for river largemouth are similar to those commonly used by lake bassers. Safety-pin spinners in ¼ and ⅛ ounce are almost always good.

Spotted Bass

The spotted bass (also known as the Kentucky bass) is underrated and overlooked. Few stream anglers realize what a great fighter it is and fewer yet spend much time fishing for it. Many streams in Kentucky, Tennessee, and West Virginia and in the Missouri and Arkansas Ozarks have both smallmouth and spotted bass, and they live in much the same rocky, faster-current areas. "Spots" also fight almost as well as smallmouth with powerful runs and high jumps. Unfortunately, stream spotted bass seldom exceed 3 pounds. Crawfish- and minnow-imitating baits similar to those preferred by smallmouth are effective in catching these close cousins. Incidentally, the name is misleading; spotted bass have much the same coloration as largemouth.

CHUBS AND FALLFISH

These two species are rarely on anybody's list of favorite fish, but they do have a few things going for them. They're easy to catch on a variety of baits, and they're very common; one or the other lives in nearly every smallmouth river on the continent. Perhaps the nicest thing about them is their value to new anglers. Anyone new to fishing always wants to catch fish, and a horde of hungry fallfish or creek chubs will provide hours of action. And besides, these fish can be eaten, creek chubs especially. In fact, I call chubs and fallfish white trout, since both vaguely resemble trout. When your friends ask what you caught last weekend, tell them "white trout."

Fallfish

The fallfish is common in many trout and bass streams of the East. It grows to 15 or 16 inches (over a pound) and will strike a variety of lures, although its small mouth calls for smaller hook sizes. Its fight, unfortunately, is pretty tepid—no high jumps or strong runs. While a few fallfish can be found in any part of a stream, the best areas are calmer and soft-bottomed pools. These areas can hold large concentrations of the fish, and in clear water some of them can often be seen suspended near the surface. Tiny plugs, spinners, spoons, jigs, and weighted flies worked slowly through these spots all elicit lots of strikes.

Chubs

Creek chubs can be thought of as the Midwest's fallfish. They inhabit eastern waters, too, but they seem to do best farther west. Creek chubs only grow to 9 or 10 inches, but they can exist in tremendous numbers. A smaller cousin, the horny-head chub (the one with the bumps on the top of its head), will occasionally be caught along with the creek chub. If a stream is too sandy for many bass, the chub will still do fine.

Chubs, like fallfish, will strike whatever they can get in their small mouths, so they are perfect for teaching inexperienced anglers how to cast and retrieve artificials properly and how to set the hook and play the fish. If you try to start beginners on trout or bass, they often become frustrated and bored with fishing because these species prove difficult to catch.

INCIDENTALS

This last category includes the drum, white bass, and mooneye — diverse species with little in common except that none is particularly common in smallmouth waters. Actually, in a certain bass stream one or more of these fish may be very common. But in the country as a whole, these three fish aren't commonly taken.

Drum

While the largemouth or walleye is prized as a valuable bonus river catch, the freshwater drum (commonly called sheephead) gets little respect, even though it grows to fair size, strikes lures well, and fights better than the walleye. The freshwater drum even looks and tastes a lot like its relative, the highly prized saltwater red drum (usually known as redfish). So what's wrong with the drum? Nothing! I catch and release many of them every year and enjoy every one. Primarily a fish of large central U.S. rivers, drum do well in silty or turbid waters; the Mississippi River in Illinois holds tremendous numbers of them, for instance. However, many much smaller rivers in the Mississippi drainage also contain substantial populations of drum. Areas below dams have huge numbers in summer. Jigs are the hands-down favorite lure for these fish, but many others will catch some.

Another nice thing about the freshwater drum is that it can be prepared so it tastes nearly the same as the delicious saltwater red drum (redfish), but you *must* preserve it properly. Drum die very easily on stringers or live wells and their flesh quickly deteriorates. Bring ice in a cooler and immediately put the fish on ice. You can easily substitute drum for the popular dish, blackened redfish. Roll fish fillets in margarine and blackened redfish seasoning mix (which can be obtained from many supermarkets) and fry in a hot skillet for two minutes per side. Delicious!

Mooneye

If the drum is unappreciated, the mooneye is unknown. Even though this unusual fish looks a little like a shad or whitefish, it isn't closely related to other species. The mooneye, like the drum, is also a native of the Mississippi drainage. It feeds heavily on insects, and in the warmer months it actually takes up feeding stations in midstream and steadily rises to the surface. If you are thinking this is a fish tailor-made for the fly fisher, you're absolutely right. The mooneye will take a dry fly as well as any trout.

If you see a fish regularly rising to something on the surface, it's probably a mooneye. At this time almost any reasonable surface presentation will do; even small bass poppers will work. But at other times the fish will strike subsurface baits like weighted flies, jigs, and even small crankbaits, so the spin fisher won't be left out. Its mouth is small and soft, so use small hooks and set the hook easy.

Mooneyes aren't huge; 2-pounders are good-sized. Their fight is only fair–no jumps or fast runs. And they aren't fantastic in the skillet since their flesh is soft (although they are very good smoked). But they are active feeders during midsummer and present a particularly exciting surface opportunity to the fly fisher.

One of many big springtime white bass taken below a dam on white jigs.

White Bass

The white bass is highly regarded in many Mid-South reservoirs, where it exists in great abundance. All across the white bass's range there are tremendous runs in the spring. In southern rivers it can start as early as late March, and in the north it can be as late as mid-May. See if some of your local rivers have an annual white bass run; it could be the fastest fishing you experience all year. It's not uncommon to catch 50 or 75 fish in a few hours! Whites nail lures furiously, fight like crazy, and reach over 2 pounds in weight—overall, a pretty respectable fish.

But the white bass isn't just a spring fling; many rivers have year-round populations. Few very small streams support a lot of summer white bass, but many canoeable rivers do. The summer or fall white bass in these smaller rivers will often be found in the largest pools. They seldom relate to any particular bottom structure, but they will often be found at the current break between fast midstream water and slow eddy water. Being notorious travelers, they will move up- and downriver during the season. And if the river has a dam, many fish will be found below it at various times of the year. By floating several miles of river containing whites you will probably find at least one pool with active fish.

Some fishers say, "Anything is good for white bass, as long as it's a white jig." This is an exaggeration, but white jigs are almost always good for these minnow-eating fish. Also good are small flashy spoons, silver-bladed in-line spinners, and bright streamer fly patterns. If the fish are really active, a jig fished quickly near the surface is deadly. Other times, fishing deeper and more slowly will produce the strikes.

Conserve the Fisheries

LONG GONE ARE THE DAYS when American (or even Canadian) sport anglers could afford to be concerned only with how many fish they can legally drag home. This outlook is particularly outdated for today's stream angler, because serious dangers threaten many of our moving waters, especially our smallmouth streams. Many of these threats can be overcome, but only if more of us get involved.

Our streams, and the fish in them, face two main threats. The most easily seen is overexploitation by sport fishing. The other danger, even more serious, is habitat deterioration and poor water quality. We need to understand both these problems so we can all do our part in overcoming them.

OVEREXPLOITATION BY SPORT FISHING

Remember the traditional pictures of the "successful" expert anglers–posing with what seems like a hundred pounds of dead fish? The decline in the printing of those fish-hog pictures is a reflection that, yes, legal sport angling can severely deplete the populations of larger fish. I'm not sure why it has taken some "experts" so long to realize this. But by now the evidence that many fine bass lakes and rivers have been harmed by angling is irrefutable. Numerous scientific studies and countless angler experiences bear this out. This rather alarming situation has finally led some fishing professionals to see the light and become promoters of catch and release.

Most streams support a very limited number of smallmouth, perhaps only several hundred per mile, and only a handful of them 1 pound or more. For comparison, some small trout streams in the East and the Midwest hold over two thousand trout per mile. Smallmouth in streams also grow slowly; the average growth rate is only 12 to 13 inches after four years. For some creeks this means a density of only three or four big bass (over 15 inches) per mile.

Not only are the numbers of larger fish limited, those that are present are often quite susceptible to angling pressure. During the prespawn period, many adult smallmouth move upstream looking for spawning habitat. If there is a dam blocking their movement, these fish will "stack up" below the dam and catch-and-kill anglers can (and do) seriously harm the population of big spawning fish. In the fall, smallmouth in many northern waterways move *downstream* to wintering areas. Once again concentrated, the large fish are very vulnerable to fishing pressure. Even in the summer months, the fish are vulnerable in many waters. If the stream becomes a series of pools separated by shallow riffles, each pool's community of bass stays put for the entire summer. Good anglers covering a waterway at this time can substantially reduce the fish in each pool, and they will not be restocked until the following year (and then only if there is a surplus of larger fish in other parts of the stream).

Over the years, I've personally witnessed the almost total depletion of large bass from popular hotspots. When word got out that certain river stretches had big smallmouth, these waters received an influx of people who kept the "nicer" fish. Sometimes in a matter of weeks the fishing in these areas was ruined; those stream sections no longer produced big bass. Ironically, many of the same people who ruined it complained later about the poor fishing. None of us can in good conscience act like this any longer.

Why Catch and Release?

So do we fish less, or hang up the fishing rod altogether? Not on your life! Rather than killing off the larger fish, simply start releasing them, so they can be caught again and again, grow larger, and

Releasing a big smallmouth to fight again.

produce more of their species. The beauty of catch and release is that it is an easy, free way all of us can directly and immediately protect and even improve our fishing. Catch and release simply means recycling the fish, releasing them without serious injury so they can be caught again. Catch and release actually creates un-limited fisheries – the number of quality fish can be permanently maintained at its upper limit. Where the numbers of bigger bass have declined due to fish-killing pressure (in other words, in most of our large and intermediate rivers), recycling the fish will bring them back to the level their habitat can support.

What about Stunting?

The question of stunting sometimes comes up when catch and release is considered. The worry is that the fish will overpopu-late in the smaller sizes and growth will be slowed because of too many fish. A few trout streams experience stunting because of large numbers of small trout. But stream smallmouth rarely do. Some waters have naturally slower growth rates because of low alkalinity, limited food sources, or short growing seasons, and they will never produce high numbers of fish or lots of big fish. Catch and release on these waters will not slow growth rates but will protect the very limited number of slow-growing big bass present.

Don't Some Released Bass Die?

Very few – as long as artificials are used exclusively. The black basses are remarkably hardy in their released survival. Caught on artificials (including barbed treble-hook lures), better than 98 percent of stream smallmouth survive if simple, minimal handling standards are followed. However, live bait does kill bass. One of the worst methods is still-fishing nightcrawlers (a common bait-fishing method on rivers). No matter how careful the angler is, many bass will swallow the hook into their throat or stomach and a significant percentage will die from internal injuries, especially if the hook is removed rather than left in the fish to dissolve. The arithmetic is this: an angler catching and releasing forty bass in a day on arti-ficials will probably not kill any fish, but that same person using bait will probably kill at least four or five bass (over 10 percent of the fish). The conclusion is obvious: on heavily fished waters the widespread use of live bait would hurt the fishing even if *all* the fish were released, while the use of artificials would have little effect on smallmouth numbers or sizes.

Besides protecting our fisheries, using artificials makes fishing itself far more interesting and active, in my opinion. The challenge of accurately working a plug or popper along a rocky bank and the excitement of seeing the strike are hard to duplicate by fishing nightcrawlers. It's rewarding to know that your fine fish taken on an artificial will almost certainly swim off to feed, grow larger, spawn – and strike your lure again in the future.

Regulations to Protect Our Sport

Some people, hoping to avoid more formal regulations limiting fish kills, propose a voluntary program. This would be fine if it worked, but unfortunately not everyone will obey good policies. Even if 80 percent of anglers voluntarily release larger fish, 15 or 20 percent probably won't. At today's level of fishing pressure and habitat restrictions, even 15 percent of the anglers can ruin the fishing on many streams.

Fortunately, "special regulations" mandating release are also good educational tools. Some special regulations for trout have been around for over a decade, and tens of thousands of anglers have been changed by them in a very positive way. Initially many were doubtful or even hostile, but as they saw with their own eyes how good fishing can be when the fish are recycled, they quickly changed their minds.

What Type of Regulations Would Be Best?

For most rivers, regulations that protect the most fish the longest would do the best job of creating a quality fishery. Probably the best (and simplest) practice would be "no kill" protection – artificials only, return all bass to the water. Regulations allowing taking only smaller fish (under 10 or 12 inches) would be the next best. Many fertile streams could stand some annual kill of small bass without noticeably reducing the number that make it to quality size (over 12 inches).

As an alternative to recycling bass, some states have put a minimum size limit on smallmouth (usually 12 inches). This fools many anglers into believing that killing fish 12 inches or larger is fine since the law specifically allows it. On hard-fished waters, such laws often result in the cropping off of most decent-sized bass and produces a stream full of runts.

Fortunately, more and more anglers and fisheries professionals are seeing the merits of recycling fish. Some wise anglers have organized themselves into groups that not only practice catch and release but also promote it. We need laws to protect our fisheries, but we also need to create social acceptance. All of us who love our sport and care about its future have to become not just practitioners but also promoters of catch and release. Talk about it to your fishing buddies. Start working on your cousin Ralph. And don't just sit quietly when you hear a guy bragging about all the big bass he brings home.

"Take the Picture Instead of the Fish"

So how do you prove that you really do catch fish? How about a photograph or two? A good picture shows not only the fish size but also the place and manner caught, and they are permanent records that can be admired forever. Taking the picture instead of the fish is an especially good practice for newer catch-and-release converts.

Taking quality photographs requires only a minimal amount of expertise. A good, easy-to-operate camera and a few basic rules will, with practice, quickly make your fishing pictures interesting and exciting. Today's pocket-sized, fully automatic 35mm. cameras are very easy to use. Small single lens reflex cameras also take tremendous pictures if you are willing to do a little more and carry a little more. Either way, make sure your camera is always handy. When you or your partner hook a good fish, immediately get the camera and any props (like a highly legible tape measure) ready and plan your picture background. It's important for the fish's well-being that it pose for only a minute or so. All the fish pictured in this book were quickly photographed and released unharmed. Even lone anglers can take pictures of their fish. Simply hold the bass as far away from you as possible and take the photo with your other hand.

Take a careful look at different photos of fish and anglers in

A nice smallie photographed using the one-person method.

national fishing magazines. From these professional shots you can gather many tips about the use of creative poses, backgrounds, lighting, and so on.

WATER QUALITY AND HABITAT

The second threat for stream smallmouth is degradation of their environment. Since this problem is so severe in some areas, I'm not going to pull any punches in discussing it. The situation is this: dozens of formerly productive rivers no longer support fishable numbers of bass, and hundreds more support less than half of the smallmouth they once did. In these streams poor water quality or habitat decline is the leading cause of reduced fish numbers.

The main causes of stream damage fall into three categories. The most obvious has been the building of big dams on waterways. The Missouri and Arkansas Ozarks and eastern mountain areas have lost hundreds of miles of stream to these concrete giants. Second, municipal and industrial pollution and residential development have also hurt many rivers across North America. Finally, harmful agricultural practices are another culprit. In fact, agricultural runoff is the main threat to healthy streams in many parts of the smallmouth's range, especially the Midwest.

Turning a stream into a reservoir obviously destroys its moving-water characteristics, but at least the lake created by the dam is suitable habitat for other fish species. And, fortunately, the building of large new dams has slowed significantly in most parts of the smallmouth's range. Municipal and industrial pollution, while still a problem on some rivers, has also been declining during the past fifteen years, largely because of the federal Clean Water Act, which came about through the efforts of environmental and conservation organizations. Some sections of streams that supported few bass or other species in the early 1970s now have fishable populations.

Urban development is a mixed scene. Many localities have adopted less destructive building ordinances. But in many other areas the push by powerful developers to build and sell homes on every available foot of stream bank continues. Heavy residential buildup right on the riverbank causes many environmental problems. The natural streamside vegetation is invariably destroyed, replaced by manicured lawns. The fish lose both food and cover sources like fallen logs, and they "gain" new sources of pesticides, fertilizers, and silt. On some streams new housing also means increased sewage pollution from individual septic tanks, since some localities have very weak laws governing septic discharge.

Besides this habitat destruction and lowered water quality, riverbank housing often leads to reduced access for the public. Even on larger streams, float fishers and canoeists no longer have places for rest or lunch stops. Uncontrolled residential development on rivers may benefit those handful of people who have homes on the river, but it most certainly hurts the 99 percent of the population who don't, not to mention the many species of fish, wildlife, and plants that are negatively affected.

The Clean Water Act also did little to lessen agricultural pollution or other stream deterioration caused by farming. In fact, during the past fifteen years, streams have suffered more than ever before from harmful farming practices. As farmland prices jumped in the 1970s, individual farmers moved to put every spare acre into cultivation. Then in the 1980s, international overproduction created a sharp farm crisis and farmers struggled to increase their crop value.

The heavy erosion on this bank was caused by planting corn too close to the stream.

They farmed closer yet to the banks of streams running through the land, even straightening the headwater tributaries, so that every inch of land could be plowed and planted. This bank-to-bank farming (especially at the headwaters) left little or no natural vegetation to hold the soil, causing heavy soil erosion and massive flooding after every rain. And with this, large amounts of toxic agricultural chemicals (pesticides and fertilizers) are washed into the waterways.

Several recent studies have shown that certain common insecticides are extremely deadly to bass. Whatever the specific causes, knowledgeable individuals generally agree that heavy planting of row crops (like corn and soybeans) right up to the stream banks, combined with heavy use of toxic chemicals, spells disaster for smallmouth. In the Midwest, from Ohio to Minnesota, once-fine rivers have suffered severely from these practices and now support only a tiny fraction of the bass they once did. Many other waterways belong on the "endangered" list; they may continue to deteriorate to the point where they too become nearly bassless. Even the pristine streams in the Ozarks and other mountain areas have suffered from harmful agricultural practices, such as clearing steep hillsides for increased cattle production.

Making Changes

We can stop these losses and turn many streams back into healthy, productive resources. Over the years, many victories have been won in the quest for cleaner water. The first thing needed is more study. I know most problems get studied to death and little ever comes of it. But in the case of our warm-water rivers more study *is* needed. Most state agencies know little about their rivers compared to what they know about their lakes or cold-water (trout) streams. Lakes and trout creeks have a vocal and active constituency. We need to become vocal too in our support for warm-water (smallmouth) streams if we want them to get the attention they deserve. Attention should focus on pinpointing specific problems and developing specific solutions for protecting individual streams.

Some other things should also be done immediately. A few towns and companies continue to dump nearly untreated sewage or toxic pollutants into our waterways in blatant disregard of the law. Anglers, canoeists, and others who use streams affected by pollution should organize and demand a halt to such abuses.

Creating natural vegetation-covered buffer strips or green-belts along a stream and its tributaries would greatly reduce agricultural or residential runoff. Streams with a good strip of natural vegetation running along their entire length are much freer of silt and chemicals and do not flood so easily. (Dramatic increases in river flows, after every rain, is a leading cause of mortality of smallmouth fry.) Even a relatively narrow buffer of only 35 or 40 feet would protect many waters.

Restoring these acres to natural use will, of course, benefit many other species besides smallmouth and other fish. In some areas of heavy farming, the remaining greenbelts along rivers or creeks support almost all the birds, mammals, and reptiles left in the area. Increasing these habitat zones will also benefit bird watchers, canoeists, campers, hunters, and many others.

Farmers should support greenbelts, too, for the benefit of future farming. Instead of pouring money into trying to grow a few more bushels on these few acres (and generating more surpluses), resources could be better allocated into developing sustainable agricultural practices on the less fragile land. Maybe individual farmers of today won't see the value of developing good land use practices, but their children will. Stopping soil erosion today will be the salvation of the farmers of tomorrow. I come from a long line of family farmers, and I personally know of the difficulties they face. To me, that only emphasizes the need for wise, long-term state and national land use policies.

Individual stream projects like bank riprapping or tree planting would also be very helpful. Erosion-control and river cleanup projects are already being done on trout streams. These local projects, sometimes by only a handful of people, often show immediate returns. This small-scale restoration work, combined with the overall goals of stream protection and catch-and-release policies, could dramatically improve our river resources.

Getting Involved

So things are happening, but stream advocates need lots more help – and that's where you and I come in. Several national environmental groups are fighting for cleaner water. Local or regional

Some members of The Smallmouth Alliance with their table display. The fish mount is a graphite replica of a released 5-pound river smallmouth. Sheldon Bolstad.

organizations focus on particular water-pollution problems. And many angling and hunting groups also increasingly see the need to get involved in environmental protection. I'll mention a few group names, just to give you an idea of the diversity and types of groups available. Many other groups not mentioned here would also be worthy of your consideration.

A few national groups worth checking into would be the Clean Water Action Project, Sierra Club, and the Federation of Fly Fishers (FFF). The FFF is not just for trout fishers; some chapters are active in protecting warm-water fisheries.

I believe the best thing for our streams would be the creation of many active, locally based, conservation-oriented smallmouth clubs. A good example is the Smallmouth Alliance. In a relatively short time it has sponsored the first Midwestern Smallmouth Symposium, researched and proposed quality smallmouth regulations, and got the state of Minnesota to implement them. The Alliance has organized river cleanups, widely promoted catch-and-release fishing, and started working with other angling and environmental groups to restore river habitat. For further information on starting local groups contact The Smallmouth Alliance at 2309 Grand Street NE, Minneapolis, MN 55418.

Joining or forming a group of this kind is not the only thing you can do. Those who already belong to a local fishing or sport club should encourage a group emphasis on catch and release and stream protection. Groups based close to rivers or creeks are important so that stream-protection efforts can be closely monitored. Even if you don't belong to any group, you can and should call lawmakers or government agencies and express your opinion. Especially when specific legislation is up for consideration, calls can have an effect.

There are many choices, but everyone who wants to see good fishing should do *something*. And once you're involved, you'll feel great. There's a particular sense of satisfaction in knowing that you are helping to ensure better fishing for yourself and others for years to come.

Index